THE POEMS OF H.

John E. Hallwas

The Poems of H.

THE LOST POET OF LINCOLN'S SPRINGFIELD

edited by JOHN E. HALLWAS

Ellis Press
Peoria, Illinois

Published by The Ellis Press, P. O. Box 1443
Peoria, Illinois 61655.

Design by David R. Pichaske

Printed by D J Graphics, Peoria,
and M & D Printers, Henry, Illinois

Preface

The discovery of a talented literary figure who has gone unrecognized for generations is always an occasion for some rejoicing. Perhaps it is especially so in this case because the midwestern frontier produced such a small amount of literature that is still worth reading.

On the other hand, too much change has taken place in American culture and literature for even the best of these poems to have the kind of popularity that they might have enjoyed more than a century ago, had they appeared in a book or magazine intended for an eastern audience. (One wonders what the position of Bryant would be in American literature if his poems had been discovered and presented to the public in our time, and without biographical information.) It can be hoped, however, that those who have learned to respond with sensitivity to the literature of earlier eras will find in this collection some poetry that provides a rewarding experience.

It is remarkable, of course, that Springfield, Illinois—rather than New York, Boston, or Cincinnati—was the place where H. lived and wrote. One would have suspected that a poet of his talent and intellectual background would not have found a suitable audience in that frontier village—and, indeed, he may have left Springfield after a few years for that reason. Or perhaps there was something special about the people of that time and place—the people to whom Lincoln later said he owed everything. In any case, this discovery will certainly not detract from the mystique that surrounds the early history of that remarkable town where the Railsplitter rose to greatness.

If this edition prompts other scholars to examine frontier newspapers, it will have served an important purpose, for the literary history of the Midwest will not be adequately understood until such research takes place. Newspapers of that era often carried original literature, and while the vast majority of it is poor, some stories, poems, and travel accounts are well worth recovering.

In regard to the editorial procedure for this volume, it should be mentioned that the few changes in the poem texts are indicated by brackets and are discussed in the Notes. Variations in spelling have not been regularized. Although punctuation is essentially the poet's (or the printer's), it has been altered freely. The surviving issues of the *Sangamo Journal* are available on microfilm and in original copies at the Illinois State Historical Library in Springfield.

Most works of scholarship are indebted to a number of professionals, and *The Poems of H.* is no exception. Special thanks are due to Ronald Rayman, who helped me locate and obtain research materials; Charles W. Mayer and Dennis J. Reader, who read and commented on early drafts of the edition; Rulon N. Smithson, who provided translations of some French and Italian lines; Roger D. Bridges, who assisted in the search through Springfield records for information about the poet; Norman Anderson, who carried on similar investigations in London; Floyd S. Barringer, who read and commented on the typescript; and David Pichaske, whose suggestions for revision and enthusiasm for the edition were both important.

John E. Hallwas

Contents

Introduction

The discovery of a hitherto unknown poet who was publishing very successful poems 150 years ago is an event of literary significance, but for the man to be living on the edge of the Illinois frontier is to enlarge our conception of what was achieved in the poetry of the early Midwest. At the present time, John Hay is generally regarded as the first midwestern poet of any national importance. No body of poetry prior to his Pike County Ballads, which appeared in the 1870's, is regarded as still worth reading or worth mentioning in literary histories. But the present collection demonstrates that a remarkably talented poet was writing on the midwestern frontier—before Hay was even born. Moreover, this literary figure produced what may be the finest poetic achievement in the Midwest before the twentieth century.

Twenty-three of the poems in this edition appeared in *The Literary Gazette* of London from 1818 to 1825 — which helps to explain the poet's unusual capability: he was a British immigrant who had begun his literary career in England. The other seventy lyrics in this volume (including all of the poet's finest works) were published in a frontier newspaper, the *Sangamo Journal* of Springfield, Illinois, from 1831 to 1846—which is the main reason for the writer's obscurity. These ninety-three items are probably not all that the poet ever wrote, but they are probably all that will ever be recovered.

I

Before discussing the poet's life and work, it is necessary to explain how his literary canon was established, for all of the poems in this edition were published anonymously. An examination of the surviving issues of Springfield's *Sangamo Journal* produced the initial discovery: that a very talented poet who signed his works with an H. had placed seventy-one poems in that newspaper between 1831 and 1846. (This was the same period when young Abraham Lincoln was struggling to launch his career in Illinois politics, and the *Sangamo Journal* was also carrying his early speeches.) Careful scrutiny of the newspaper issues and other local records from that period of time produced no hint as to the poet's identity. However, it was clear from his poems that he was an English immigrant.

Fortunately, a footnote to one of the lyrics, "Sonnet: To a Young Lady Musing" (which appeared in May of 1832), indicated that it was "First published in the London Literary Gazette."[1] A search through the issues of that journal eventually disclosed that the sonnet had appeared in volume five, published in 1819. However, the poem was printed with no name or initial beneath it. Other lyrics signed with an H. were found in *The Literary Gazette,* but none seemed at all similar to those in the *Sangamo Journal.* (It was evident, in fact, that at least two British poets—neither of whom had interests and capabilities akin to those of the Springfield author—signed their contributions to that journal with an H. during the 1820's.) On the other hand, several sonnets that were signed J.H. were very similar to sonnets in the Springfield newspaper. Altogether, during 1819-1822 ten sonnets had been published in the *Gazette* under the initials J.H. Most of them were simply entitled "Sonnet," which was the title used by H. for poems of that kind in the *Sangamo Journal.* Moreover, a few had headnotes that were quotations from British, French, or Italian authors, which was also true of many sonnets in the American newspaper. Beyond that, one poem in the *Gazette,* "Sonnet: Winter," described the pleasures of the winter fireside in terms that were very similar to a lyric in the *Sangamo Journal* entitled "Winter Nights," and another sonnet from the *Gazette* ("Vain thoughts, vain hopes, and fond desires are fled,") bore some resemblance to a sonnet in the newspaper also ("To struggle on, to struggle on for aye,"). Furthermore, the contemplation of death was a common element in both groups of sonnets. For these reasons, it was apparent that J.H. of *The Literary Gazette* and H. of the *Sangamo Journal* were the same man.

Once these sonnet resemblances had been noted, the *Gazette* was searched for other, similar sonnets that had *not* been signed with the initials J.H.—because "Sonnet: To a Young Lady

Musing" had already demonstrated that the poet occasionally used no initials at all. One unsigned poem, "Sonnet: The Poet Laments the Death of His Cat, Scracco," which appeared in 1821, was undoubtedly by the same poet, for in the previous year J.H. had published "Sonnet: The Poet Praises His Cat, Scracco." Also, three sonnets that appeared in the British journal during 1818 were very similar to the sonnets signed J.H. These three were closely related to each other in subject matter—the poet, troubled by the loss of his beloved, was unsuccessfully seeking solace in the natural world—and so they were unquestionably by the same hand. More importantly, like most of the sonnets signed J.H. and H., they were simply entitled "Sonnet," were written in a smooth yet vigorous style, and—in two cases—had foreign language headnotes (one in French, the other in Italian). Also, the speaker's struggle against despair in these poems was similar to the subject matter of a poem by J.H.: "Sonnet: To Melancholy." Hence, with confidence these three unsigned sonnets were ascribed to the poet who in 1819 began to sign J.H. to his contributions in the *Gazette.*

That J.H. was, in fact, sending poetry to that journal in 1818 is evident from the column entitled "To Correspondents," in which the editor made public comments to authors who had sent in poems for publication or had sent inquiries about submitting poetry. In the late summer and fall of that year, three messages for J.H. appeared: "If J.H. pleases to communicate what he alludes to, it shall be attended to, as may then seem most agreeable to our plan"; "J.H.'s packet came to hand, and lies for consideration"; "J.H. The Literary Gazette is more than full at present in the department specified."[2]

Also, two other unsigned sonnets ("Sweet Spring, thy young and soft love-beaming eye" and "Whilst on the couch of pain and sorrow laid,") were identified as the poet's because they were in his characteristic style, were simply entitled "Sonnet," and had headnotes from Italian authors that were identical to headnotes used for poems published in the *Sangamo Journal.* Yet another unsigned sonnet ("Now through the air the western breezes play,") was ascribed to the poet for similar reasons: it was entitled "Sonnet," had a headnote from the poetry of William Drummond —as did one of the J.H. sonnets—and was similar in style and subject matter to the sonnet on spring that was just mentioned.

Four other poems signed J.H. that were not sonnets were also located in the *Gazette*. "The Spectre" is a thirty-two-line lyric about a grieving man whose dead beloved appears to him in the night. It is, then, thematically related to the three unsigned sonnets of 1818 mentioned above. Moreover, the speaker's struggle with despair links the poem with "Sonnet: To Melancholy" as well.

"Hodge" is a 132-line comparison of country and city life. Although it is strikingly different from the other J.H. poems, this lyric contains one line that is very similar to a line in a *Sangamo Journal* poem entitled "Lines on the Approach of Winter," and two other lines that are almost identical to lines in a *Sangamo Journal* poem entitled "The Independent Philosopher." Also, like "Sonnet: Winter" by J.H. and "Winter Nights" by H., "Hodge" describes the pleasures of the fireside in winter, and like "The Remonstrance" and "Sonnet" ("The sullen hours on leaden pinions fly,") in the *Sangamo Journal,* "Hodge" refers to a common cat's name, "Grimalkin" (or "Grey-malkin"). Like T.S. Eliot, the poet was apparently fond of cats.

"Culloden" is a thirty-line poem that memorializes the famous battlefield near Inverness where the Scots, under the leadership of Pretender Charles Edward Stuart, were defeated by the British in 1746. Although the subject matter is not similar to that of any other lyric by the author, it is worth noting that he later indicated in a *Sangamo Journal* poem that he was of Scottish descent.

The fourth poem, "To Poverty," is a sixteen-line lyric in which the speaker reflects on his impoverished circumstances. However, it is not by the same man, for the journal's editor added a footnote to the poem that identified the author as John Hartnoll, a youth whose first poem (a book-length elegy) had just appeared in print.[3] In other words, the editor was evidently making a distinction between the J.H. who had written "To Poverty" and the poet who had been publishing items in the *Gazette* under those initials for the previous two or three years.

Also located in the *Gazette* were two brief translations, or literary adaptations, that were signed J.H. The earlier one, "Lines/Tradotto," is an English couplet that is followed by a six-line lyric in Italian that is derived from it. The other item, entitled "Epigram," is a four-line translation for which the source is given: "From 'Le Ramelet Moundi' by Godelin, a poet who wrote in the dialect of Thoulouse, early in the 17th century." Although it is possible that either or both of those were written by John Hartnoll—since they appeared in 1821 and 1825 respectively, after he had published his first poem in the *Gazette*—it is far more likely that they were the work of that J.H. who had written sonnets for the British journal since 1818. The latter's familiarity with French and Italian is demonstrated time and again by his use of poem titles and headnotes from those languages. Moreover, there is no evidence that John Hartnoll published more than one lyric in the *Gazette,* while the other J.H. was a constant contributor.

Hence, a search through the London *Literary Gazette* located eighteen sonnets, one satirical poem ("Hodge"), two other lyrics ("The Spectre" and "Culloden"), and two brief translations that were written by a poet who usually signed his works J.H. but occasionally did not sign them at all, and who was undoubtedly the same man who later published poems in the *Sangamo Journal.* Furthermore, one of the 1819 poems by J.H., "Sonnet: The Poet Praises His Cat, Scracco," proved to be virtually identical to a lyric in the Springfield newspaper, "Sonnet: The Poet Praises His Cat," which appeared in February of 1832. The latter had not previously been counted among the newspaper lyrics by H. because it was signed "Another Bachelor." (Some other Springfield poet who signed his work "A Bachelor" had started a controversy about cats—in an issue of the *Sangamo Journal* that does not survive—and so H. decided to reprint his cat poem from *The Literary Gazette.* He evidently signed it "Another Bachelor" instead of H. to show the similarity between himself and the other unmarried poet, who had started the controversy.) Hence, *The Literary Gazette* and the *Sangamo Journal* have two poems in common: "Sonnet: To a Young Lady Musing" and "Sonnet: The Poet Praises His Cat [Scracco]." The reprinted versions of these sonnets are not counted among the ninety-three items that make up the poet's canon, although the texts are given in the Notes to this edition.

II

At the present time, very little is known about the poet. The fact that he was publishing lyrics in *The Literary Gazette* by 1818 indicates that he must have been born in the later eighteenth century. He was raised in Cornwall, as he reveals in a lyric called "Taur Arthur," which focuses on a rock along the southwestern coast of England that he often saw as a child. A reference to Tintagel Castle, the legendary residence of King Arthur, in the same poem locates his home area on Cornwall's northern coast, near Boscastle.

It is also apparent that he lived in or near London as a young man, for one of his early sonnets ("There came to me a poor and care-worn clerk,") displays his familiarity with the famous legal societies of that city, the Inns of Court. He specifically mentions Lincoln's Inn, Gray's Inn, and The Temple. (The last of these refers to two different legal societies located in the same area. The Inner Temple and The Middle Temple.) Moreover, the same poem clearly suggests that he had once been associated with one of the Temple societies — "there I draw out rhymes where erst I drew out pleas." Other poems by H. contain recollections of the Thames River.

His lyrics also suggest that he had received a good education. He either quotes from or refers to the following writers: Homer, Ovid, Horace, Dante, Petrarch, Hafez, Tasso, Spenser, Shakespeare, Drummond, Godelin, Milton, Butler, Deshoulieres, Filicaia, Boileau, Pope, Metastasio, Gray, Anstey, Burns, Scott, Byron, and Moore. He was also acquainted with Hindu scriptures, classical and Norse mythology, and Arthurian legend. Moreover, he demonstrates a considerable knowledge of Italian and French (since a number of his poems have titles or headnotes in those languages), and he uses a little Latin in "Cauld Comfort," "Huyler's Ghost," and "Bards and Reviewers."

Since the poet already knew Italian and French before he began writing lyrics for *The Literary Gazette* in 1818—as his poetic headnotes indicate—he had probably traveled to Italy and France before that time. He had certainly done some traveling on the continent before immigrating to America, for in "Il Melancolico per Amore" (published in the *Sangamo Journal* in 1832) he recalls a visit to Italy, and in a sonnet ("There is a charm in foreign lands to be,") published in 1838, he refers to wandering in Spain and Italy. The subject matter of "Culloden" suggests that he may also have visited Scotland sometime prior to 1822, when it appeared.

Although he does not mention when he left England for the United States, it is clear that he had traveled in eastern North America before he came to Springfield. A lyric entitled "The Exile" mentions that he was "Along the Mohawk's pleasant stream," "By Niagara's giant falls," and in "deep Ontario," while a sonnet ("O thou shrill warbler of the woody wild,") published in 1833 refers to his acquaintance with the Schuylkill, Hudson, and St. Lawrence rivers.

Although the date of his emigration is unknown, the poet does indicate why he left England — at least in a general sense. In "To 'The Prairie Bard'" he explains, "liberty is aye my creed . . ./For her I left the island foggy." This is the only indication that restrictions upon his freedom motivated his emigration. The poem also reveals that he was of Scottish descent, for, as he remarks, "in my cap I wear the thistle [flower]," the heraldic and national emblem of Scotland.

Since Springfield was founded in 1821, the poet could have arrived there almost any time after that year and before the fall of 1831, when he began to write poetry for the *Sangamo Journal.* However, the brief poetic translation entitled "Epigram" did not appear in *The Literary Gazette* until 1825. If indeed the J.H. who signed that piece was the same man who published many lyrics in the *Gazette* from 1818 to 1822, he was probably still in London when "Epigram" was published. At the same time, in the preface to "Huyler's Ghost," H. refers to an acquaintance (Old Huyler) of the Springfield area in terms that suggest they knew each other for a considerable time before the poem was written (January of 1832). Thus, it is likely that H. was in Springfield during the late 1820's.

Evidence reveals that the poet continued to travel after moving to Springfield. "A Night on the Prairie," published in May of 1833, describes a night spent in the "barren wild," but more impor-

tantly, a preface to the lyric by the editor of the *Sangamo Journal*
asserts that the poet "is still 'in search of adventure' somewhere in
the North Western Territory." This suggests that H. very much
enjoyed traveling in the West and may often have done so.
Another poem, which is simply called "Sonnet" (and which also
appeared in May of 1832), begins by referring to the poet's return
home—probably from the travels described by the *Journal* editor:

> Again upon these wilds—my weary feet,
> From Mississippi's farthest, fairest strand,
> Seek the green sward, in other days so sweet,
> When first I rambled here, a *stranger* in the land.

Other poems, notably "Travelling the Prairie in Summer" and
"Sonnet" ("Fierce overhead the fervid dog-star reigns"), which
appeared in the summer of 1832, suggest that he was already
familiar with the rigors of traveling in the West by that time.

By 1845 H. had moved to the South, for he says in a sonnet
published in October of that year, "From southern shores to
Sangamo I come—/Fair Sangamo that whilom was my home. . . ."
He may have moved to New Orleans, which was not only located
on the southern shore of America but had the kind of European-
ized culture that he would have enjoyed. It is impossible to
determine exactly when H. left Springfield, but more than half of
his poems were published in the *Sangamo Journal* between
December of 1831, when his first lyric appeared, and July of 1833.
After that time, four years passed before another of his poems was
printed there (although some issues of the newspaper from the
1833-1837 period are missing, and so this calculation could be
inaccurate). Three lyrics appeared in 1837; three others appeared
in 1838, and six more were published in 1839. Thus, it is possible
that H. was back in Springfield during those years. However, he
probably left for good in 1833 or 1834 and thereafter simply
mailed poems to the newspaper. After four more years had
passed, a single lyric was published in the *Journal* in 1843, and so
it is likely that he was not in touch with Springfield during the

1838-1843 period. In any case, five lyrics appeared in the fall of
1845 and twelve in the months of January, February, and March of
1846. His last known lyric was published on March 26, 1846. This
great increase in published poems during a six-month period was
undoubtedly the result of his visit to Sangamon County in the fall
of 1845.

Very little is known about the poet's life in Springfield—he is
not mentioned in the surviving city records of the 1820's and
1830's—but fortunately, he revealed his occupation twice during
1832. In the long preface to "Sonnet to the Frogs" H. depicts
himself as the taverner of Jabez Capps' Grocery (general store and
bar). As he puts it, he can be found "in that sanctuary of drink and
dry goods yclept Capps' Grocery—surrounded . . . all the day long
by the brawling votaries of Bacchus, or whiskey rather, for that is
the proper name of the Sucker-god of guzzle. . . ." And this
impression is confirmed by his preface to "Huyler's Ghost," in
which he discusses the town drunk, who evidently had recently
died. H. reflects at one point, "How many a gill have I drawn
thee. . . ." Moreover, in the poem itself, Huyler's ghost appears to
the poet, and the latter pours him drink after drink in a comic
reenactment of their former relationship. Jabez Capps had come
to Illinois from London in 1819, and so it is possible that he had
known the poet there and had subsequently written to him about
settling in Springfield.

H's poems also reveal some aspects of his personal life. It has
already been stated that a few early lyrics describe his grief over
the death of his beloved. He also mentions in "To 'The Prairie
Bard'" that he is "a single man," and in "The Remonstrance" he
declares that he is too old for love—"love with me has had his
day"—and then goes on to satirize old bachelors like himself.
Since he was at least approaching middle age when these poems
were written (1832), he probably never did marry. Moreover, "Le
Solitaire" indicates that he prized his solitude, and in "Winter
Nights" he portrays himself as content to sit alone before his
fireside (as he did also in his early poem, "Sonnet: Winter").

He was obviously interested in nature, for he wrote several
poems on the seasons and others on frogs, wolves, and whippoor-
wills. In "Vernal Musings" he describes his thoughts while on a

walk through the natural world near Springfield, and in a similar
poem entitled "To the Frogs" he indicates that such solitary
strolls were common. Likewise, a few of the sonnets published in
The Literary Gazette reveal the poet's practice of taking walks in
the countryside.

It is also apparent from his Springfield poems that H. enjoyed
people—and, indeed, as a taverner, he must have spent consider-
able time in the company of others. In his preface to "Sonnet to the
Frogs" he mentions winning a jew's harp "from a New England
pedlar in a fair contest of *hyme* singing," which suggests that he
was outgoing and ready for a good time. That he liked even the
town drunk in evident—as mentioned above—from the preface to
"Huyler's Ghost." Moreover, poems like "To the Small Beer
Poets," "Bards and Reviewers," and "Lament for the Small Beer
Poets" indicate that he saw himself not as a solitary writer but as
the foremost figure among poets in the Springfield area, while
"To 'The Prairie Bard'" is a convivial verse letter to a capable poet
in nearby Jacksonville. Also, in "On the Arrival of the First Steam
Boat," H. mentions that his poetry earned him a new pair of
breeches, presented by his local admirers (lines 129-31). Hence, it
is possible to say that the poet valued alike the pleasures of
companionship and the satisfactions of solitude.

The reference to receiving breeches as a gift from his admirers
also raises the question of how highly regarded H. was in the
Springfield area. As early as January of 1832, the *Sangamo
Journal* editor, Simeon Francis, referred to him as "our inimitable
bard."[4] During the next month, an anonymous poet who men-
tioned the beauty of the prairies also paid H. a compliment by
saying, "The theme's too high for me to raise./Come Mr. H. and
sing its praise."[5] And in May of that year, two poems entitled "To
H." were carried by the *Journal.* One was signed "Puer," and the
writer mentioned that he had often read H's poems, although he
had never been to Springfield. He also called H. the "Master
rhymer of the Journal," praised his Scots dialect—"My ear the
difference scarce discerns/Between your Scotch an' that o'
Burns"—and encouraged him to continue writing:

Rhyme on, my lad, ye'll grace your station—
Amuse the lan', improve the nation.

Ye've got thysel' a wondrous name,
'Twill live in everlastin' fame.[6]

Of course, the final line in this passage is ironic, in view of the poet's subsequent obscurity, even in the Springfield area. The other poem was signed "Prairie Bard," and it had been provoked by an earlier lyric written by H., as the discussion of "To 'The Prairie Bard'" below indicates. In any case, it was composed in Jacksonville, about thirty-five miles away, which proves that the poet had some following in that town. Indeed, The Prairie Bard claimed that H. charmed the people in Jacksonville with his "weekly ditty."[7] As these references demonstrate, the poet received a good deal of praise from residents of central Illinois who read the *Sangamo Journal.*

One final biographical matter is worth considering: would H. have known of Lincoln, or Lincoln have known of him? Since the young Railsplitter did not move to Springfield until 1837, after H. was gone, we can be certain that Lincoln did not come to the poet's attention while the latter resided in town. On the other hand, when H. was writing his longest and most original poems for the *Sangamo Journal*—in the early 1830's—Lincoln was living at New Salem, less than twenty miles away. He must have read at least some of H's poems at that time. Lincoln was, of course, interested in poetry himself as a young man, and he left a couple of lyrics among his literary remains. It is also possible that Lincoln met H. during the latter's visit to Springfield in 1845, for by that time Lincoln was a prominent lawyer and local politician, and the two men must have had some friends in common—including newspaper editor Simeon Francis. Even if they did not meet, Lincoln would almost certainly have read some of the lyrics that H. published in the *Sangamo Journal* in 1845 and 1846. Hence, works by the finest poet of the early Midwest must have been a part of the young legislator's reading, probably at both New Salem and Springfield.

While very little is known about the poet—not even his name— enough details have been recovered to allow the formulation of some important questions. Where did he receive his apparently fine education? What was his occupation in London? What was the nature of his association with the Inner or Middle Temple? When did he travel to Italy and Spain? What kind of restrictions on his liberty caused him to emigrate? Why did he settle in Springfield— when the East Coast would have been a more logical choice for a Londoner with literary interests? Why did he publish so much poetry—including his most significant achievements—in Springfield? Where else did he publish lyrics in England and America besides *The Literary Gazette* and the *Sangamo Journal*? Where did he go after he left Springfield in 1833 or 1834? And, perhaps the most provoking question of all, why did he persistently conceal his identity in print—especially in a frontier village like Springfield, which had perhaps 900 people when he began writing for the *Sangamo Journal*? Unless the poet's name is discovered, so that biographical research can begin, most of these questions are not likely to be answered.

III

Before discussing the poetry of H., two preliminary questions need to be considered: should he be viewed as an American author, and what was the level of poetic achievement in the West at the time he began writing for the *Sangamo Journal*? The first of these is not as easy to resolve as one might think. On the one hand, he was born and raised in England; he began his literary career there, and he occasionally refers to that country in his later poems as "my native isle" or "my home." However, he did immigrate to America; he calls himself "Another western pioneer" in "To 'The Prairie Bard,'" and he never expresses any intention of returning to England, although he longs to see the people and places he once knew. Since the poet indicates in "To 'The Prairie Bard'" that he left England because "liberty is aye my creed," he evidently felt that he could not return there—although he may have wanted to at times—without compromising his values. In this respect, his situation resembles that of another British immigrant to Illinois, Morris Birkbeck, who expresses his love for his "native country" in "Letter V" of *Letters from Illinois* (1818) but also views England as repressive in comparison to America.[8]

The general content of H's literary canon does not offer a clear answer to the question either. Aside from his poems in *The Literary Gazette*, several of the poet's later lyrics are based on recollections of his life in England, and "Taur Arthur" even displays his sense of heritage as a British poet from Cornwall. On the other hand, the vast majority of his surviving poems were written in America, including all of his finest achievements. Also, most of his poems which evoke a specific locale are concerned with the American frontier, which he wrote about not as a visitor but as a resident. More importantly, the poet's conception of himself as "The Sangamo Bard" (the poet of Sangamon County) in poems like "Bards and Reviewers" and "On the Arrival of the First Steam Boat" indicates that he considered himself an American poet—at least in the early 1830's. In fact, "Bards and Reviewers" finds him defending his chosen role as a poet of the western frontier.

Hence, there is considerable justification for viewing him as a writer in both the British and American literary traditions. Within the former tradition, he is the most capable—and perhaps the only significant—author to reside in and reflect the American frontier, and within the latter tradition, he is the most valuable midwestern poet of his time.

Since H's vivid depiction of his experience in the early Midwest is central to his importance as a poet in either case, and since he sought to create and promote poetry indigenous to that region, it would be worthwhile to discuss briefly the quality of poetry produced there up to the time he began writing. As one might expect, the vast majority of midwestern lyrics written before 1831—or, for that matter, before the Civil War—were exceedingly poor. Vague language and metronomic versification were widely employed to treat familiar topics and express commonplace notions. Hence, American literary scholarship has justifiably ignored the poetry of the early Midwest.[9] However, some poets were capable of producing readable, if undistinguished, verse.

One of the most widely read midwestern poems of the 1820's, Micah Flint's "Lines on the Mounds in the Cahokia Prairie, Illinois," offers an example of the best poetry written in the region before H's poems appeared. It was first published in Timothy Flint's (his father's) *Recollections of the Last Ten Years in the Valley of the Mississippi* (1826). The opening stanzas are as follow:

The sun's last rays were fading from the west,
The deepening shade stole slowly o'er the plain,
The evening breeze had lulled itself to rest,
And all was silence,—save the mournful strain
With which the widowed turtle wooed in vain
Her absent lover to her lonely nest.

Now, one by one emerging to the sight,
The brighter stars assumed their seats on high;
The moon's pale crescent glowed serenely bright,
As the last twilight fled along the sky,
And all her train, in cloudless majesty,
Were glittering on the dark blue vault of night.

I lingered, by some soft enchantment bound,
And gazed enraptured on the lovely scene;
From the dark summit of an Indian mound
I saw the plain outspread in living green,
Its fringe of cliffs was in the distance seen,
And the dark line of forest sweeping round.

I saw the lesser mounds which round me rose;
Each was a giant heap of mouldering clay;
There slept the warriors, women, friends, and foes,
There side by side the rival chieftains lay;
And mighty tribes, swept from the face of day,
Forgot their wars and found a long repose.

Ye mouldering relics of departed years,
Your names have perished; not a trace remains,
Save where the grass-grown mound its summit rears
From the green bosom of your native plains.
Say, do your spirits wear oblivion's chains?
Did death forever quench your hopes and fears?[10]

The language is deliberately "poetic," and the lines have very little rhythmic vitality. The subject matter may have been new to American literature, but the poet treated it in a conventional way, making his experience typical rather than unique. Still, this lyric is better than most midwestern poetry published before the Civil War.

Not long after Flint's poem appeared, James Hall, who had moved to Illinois from Pennsylvania, became the most well-known literary figure in the West. His short stories were entertaining but otherwise undistinguished, and his lyrics were even less valuable. For example, "The Prairie," which Hall published in his *Illinois Monthly Magazine* in September of 1831, opens with the following stanzas:

> The prairie was clad in its richest array,
> It's brightest of scarlet, and gayest of green;
> And the sun seemed to pause in his luminous way,
> And to sparkle with joy o'er the beautiful scene.
> The flowers—though florists will hardly agree
> To a doctrine so strange and so novel to them—
> Were blushing, and bowing, and making as free
> As if each had a heart in its delicate stem.[11]

The heavy four-stress rhythm overpowers the lines, and the pathetic fallacy is a poor substitute for the unique reality of an unbroken Illinois prairie. (It is interesting to reflect that in 1833 William Cullen Bryant combined Flint's subject matter with Hall's to produce "The Prairies," which became the most famous American poem about the western frontier.)

In any case, Hall had difficulty getting poetry and fiction of even "respectable" quality for his periodical—the first literary magazine published west of Ohio—and so he was forced to fill out issues with his own short stories, poems, and articles. In 1833 he gave up the venture and moved to Cincinnati, where poets like William D. Gallagher and Otway Curry were producing lyrics, the best of which were not much better than Hall's own efforts. Yet by that time, less than seventy-five miles from Hall's home in Vandalia, H. had already published lyrics that were clearly the

most distinctive poetic achievements written in the early Mid-
west.

IV

H's poems have been divided into several groups for this
edition, to help display the range of his capability as a poet. The
first of them is Early Poems, which contains the twenty-three
items that he wrote from 1818 to 1825 for *The Literary Gazette.*
Those lyrics constitute his achievement before immigrating to
America, and while none is outstanding, a few are sufficiently well
written to make enjoyable reading.

Of the poet's 1818 sonnets, two depict him as woeful because
his expectations of love were thwarted, and the other indicates
that his beloved was taken from him by death. The latter, "I seek
the fields, the woods, and gentle streams," is best of the three, for
it reflects the poet's struggle to cope with his grief. He evidently
never got over the loss of his beloved, for in a few of the later
poems he recalls her untimely death ("To the Small Beer Poets,"
lines 108-17; "The Roses," lines 27-42; and "Lines" ["Dark o'er
my brow the vanished years"], lines 7-8). In others, it is apparent
that her absence from his life contributes to his dejection ("Taur
Arthur," lines 12-28) and to his wistful longing for the past ("Many
Years Ago").

Other sonnets that appeared in 1819, 1820, and 1822 reveal
that the poet was subject to fits of sadness and depression.
"Sonnet: To Melancholy" is one of those, and it closes with the
following couplet: "oft as I go forth in gloom and care,/I meet that
wizard, dark and fell Despair!" H. often personified emotions in
his early sonnets, but he still managed to achieve a certain
intensity—as "Sonnet" ("Vain thoughts, vain hopes, and fond
desires are fled") demonstrates.

He also turned his attention to other, more pleasant subjects
after 1818. "Sonnet: Winter," mentioned above as being similar to
"Winter Nights" in the *Sangamo Journal,* effectively describes his
enjoyment of the fireside "when cold and wind prevail," and two
less successful sonnets on spring convey the pleasures of that
season. In 1819 and 1820 he wrote sonnets about his cat, Scracco,

and then in 1821 he published a related sonnet that was addressed to a mouse, whose presence reminded him that his cat was no longer alive. The latter illustrates H's talent for providing rhythmic variety in his poems:

> I will not hurt thee, sleek and gentle mouse,
> Although you nib my cheese and spoil my bread.
> No cat have I to scare thee from the house,
> For she, alas! poor Scracco, now is dead.
> Then fly not, little prowler, but remain,
> And take the bits which from my table fall.
> You're very welcome, nor will I complain
> If, in a hungry fit, you eat up all.
> Think not that Jemmy will thy life destroy;
> (Jemmy is he who wears the scowling brow.)
> His look, indeed, is stern, but then, my boy,
> His heart's not wholly flint, I do avow.
> So eat, and stuff they little jacket well;
> Feasts do not often come, that I can tell.

This is one of his better early lyrics, and it may have been influenced by Burns' "To a Mouse." Like that famous poem, it conveys the speaker's sensitivity to the mouse's situation. (The name "Jemmy" evidently refers to the poet's dog.)

Another early lyric worth reading is "Culloden," which offers two views of the famous battlefield where Pretender Charles Edward Stuart and his Scottish supporters were defeated by the British, led by the Duke of Cumberland. The opening verse paragraph depicts the 1746 battle itself, where "man and babe and woman fall,/Till one wide ruin covers all." Then the poem closes with a second description of the location—now strangely quiet and empty after seventy-five years have passed:

> The pale moon rises o'er the scene
> As if no battle there had been—
> And the grey morn peeps gaily forth
> Where sleep the bravest of the North.

There is no lyric similar to this one among the *Sangamo Journal*
poems, but the poet's facility with the closed octosyllabic couplet
form—so evident in "Culloden"—is central to his later achieve-
ment in America.

The only early poem which is at all like the satires that H. wrote
for the Springfield newspaper is "Hodge." It is not entirely
satirical, for the first ten stanzas describe the satisfactions of
country life, and the name Hodge is used to denote the country-
man of good character. In the rest of the poem, H. satirizes life in
the city (London), where "The maidens flaunt/And gallivaunt,/
Bedizen'd out so fine," and "The single man/Looks pale and
wan,/Th' effect of early riot." Although the unusual aabccb stanza
form (with the third and sixth lines having six syllables and the
other lines having only four) was not employed in the later satires,
it was used again in "The Independent Philosopher," which ap-
peared in the *Sangamo Journal* in 1845.

The lyrics from *The Literary Gazette* do not add up to a poetic
achievement of any importance. However, they reveal that the
poet was a competent sonneteer who had a talent for creating
vigorous rhythms and at least some interest in working with other
lyric forms. It is also apparent that he had been influenced by
literary developments of the Romantic Period, for he often
dramatized his emotional condition—especially when coping with
his beloved's death, reacting to the influence of nature, and
reflecting on the deterioration of his youthful outlook. While
"Hodge" is partly satirical, it offers no intimation of the poet's
later achievement in comical-satirical poetry. In other words, it is
apparent that his literary craftsmanship matured considerably
between the early 1820's and the fall of 1831, when he began
writing for the *Sangamo Journal.*

H's American satires—which also sometimes include non-
satirical (humorous or serious) elements—were published in the
Springfield newspaper between December of 1831 and June of
1833, with all but one appearing by April of 1832. Hence, his
period of production as a satirist was rather brief. Six of the nine
poems are over 100 lines long, and a couple run to more than 200
lines. For this reason, the satires amount to more than one third of
the poet's surviving lines (1154 out of 3219), and Satirical Poems

is by far the longest section of this edition. Since those poems are predominant among the early contributions to the *Sangamo Journal,* and most of them deal with frontier culture, it is likely that H's new environment prompted him to produce satires rather than sonnets.

Poetic satires by several British writers were known to the poet. To provide a headnote for an early sonnet, he quoted a line from Christopher Anstey, whose very popular epistolary novel in verse, *The New Bath Guide* (1766), satirized aspects of life at Bath. Also, in "Bards and Reviewers" he refers to "The ease and elegance of Pope," and he mentions Butler's *Hudibras.* Moreover, the poem's title reveals that he must have been acquainted with Byron's *English Bards and Scots Reviewers.*

But the most obvious influence on H's satires came from Burns. The first three that he published—"Hame's the Best Place A'ter A'," "Cauld Comfort," and "To 'The Prairie Bard'"—are in Scots dialect, which suggests that he looked consciously to Burns as a model before starting to write his satirical poetry. Furthermore, "Hame's the Best Place A'ter A'" is a comical-satirical narrative that focuses on local culture and employs vigorous colloquial language, all of which is characteristic of Burns' poetry. Also, the devil, who is the poem's central figure, is referred to as "Auld Nickieben," a borrowing from the final stanza of Burns' "Address to the Deil." The second of his satires, "Cauld Comfort," has a verse headnote—"Gie him gude drink/Until he wink"—which is taken from the headnote to Burns' "Scotch Drink." And as the title of the third satire indicates, it is a verse epistle, which is a common poetic form in the canon of Burns. Aside from those three satires, the only other Scots poem that H. published in the *Journal* is a short, humorous verse epistle entitled "On the Present of a Pincushion by a Lady," which appeared in August of 1832. (However, a brief section of "Bards and Reviewers" is also in Scots.)

Among the poet's satires are some of his most unique achievements. As mentioned above, "Hame's the Best Place A'ter A'" applies the style and technique of Burns to American subject matter, which makes the poem very unusual. It is also worth noting that the story itself (without the satirical elements) is related to the American tall tale tradition that thrived in New England and the Old Southwest: the devil visits Sangamon County, where he finds the cold winters harder to put up with than the heat of hell. The folk culture of Illinois may have supplied the idea for this narrative, for the previous winter had been the exceedingly severe Winter of the Deep Snow.

The vigorous rhythms of this poem are nowhere more evident than at the beginning, where the devil addresses his comrades in colloquial language—which had not previously appeared in American poetry, in Scots dialect or otherwise:

> Auld Nickieben ('twas in warm weather)
> Assembled a' the de'ils thegither;
> "An' weal enow," Auld Sooty cried,
> "My louvin chiels, ye've stew'd an' fried—
> You've had a bellyfu' o' brunstane,
> An' hard your fate as ony whunstane.
> I'll jist agen, as ance afore,
> My luck in other realms explore,
> An' aiblins, I moen find a biggin,
> Mair cozie, chiels, for us to ligin."

When the devil arrives on the frontier, he runs across a parson, doctor, and attorney, who become his cronies. They are briefly satirized by the poet. Later in the narrative, after the three inept professionals marry and settle down, the satirical focus shifts to the devil's relationships with women. In between these sections Old Nick comments briefly on Springfield's rowdies:

> The de'il beheld wi' joy the rabble
> Drink, swear an' fight, an' gouge, an' scrabble.
> "Weal done," he cried, "ye're jist yoursel',
> An' like my ain sweet babes o' hell.
> I fegs, I love ye quite as weal."

The implication, of course, is that Springfield is similar to hell, at least in this regard. While not a superb poem, "Hame's the Best Place A'ter A'" is an original and amusing narrative.

Also unusual is "Cauld Comfort," an anti-temperance satire. The temperance cause was very important on the frontier, and many Illinois newspapers regularly carried stories, poems, and articles that pointed out the evils of liquor and advocated temperance as a panacea for the ills of society. There were probably temperance sympathizers in Springfield from the very beginning, but they seem to have organized and become vocal in 1830 or 1831. In the years that followed, they even sponsored a newspaper dedicated to the abolition of liquor: the *Western Washingtonian.*

On the other hand, there were many people in town—and elsewhere in Illinois—who disliked the temperance cause, but they usually did not say so in print. However, H. had more than one inducement to write "Cauld Comfort." First of all, he was the taverner at Jabez Capps' Grocery, and so he undoubtedly wanted to defend his livelihood and that of his friend and employer. At the same time, Burns had celebrated liquor in "Scots Drink" and had praised the social value of drinking in "To John Goldie," and so H. had an important poetic precedent for taking the stand that he did. And finally, it is clear from the poem that H. viewed temperance as a form of extremism that fostered the breakdown of civility and human concern.

"Cauld Comfort" is written as if it were a public address on the temperance issue, with the poet attacking both the logic and the inhumanity of the anti-liquor crusaders, as the following lines demonstrate:

Suppose I meet a friend maist dear,
Wham I've not seen for many a year,
Must I sic friend at ance gae slau'ter,
An' gie him water, water, water?
Wad ye turn a' the warld to Quakers,
An' mak' men hypocrites an' Shakers?
An' know ye not, ye daft moon-rakers,
That those things which forbidden are
Each mother's son langs for the mair?

His reference to slaughtering a friend and his puns on "Quakers"

and "Shakers" reinforce the theme of inhumanity, as he points out
that the temperance cause also promotes hyprocrisy. Elsewhere
in the poem, he views the temperance advocates as lacking in
Christian values (they are "heathen" and have "nae mercie"), and
thus, as he indicates at the outset, they are mistakenly following
the devil. In terms of human relationships, they are "Cauld"
(cold)—like the water they recommend as a substitute for whis-
key—or, in other words, they are opposed to the warmth of human
concern. In contrast, the speaker is vividly characterized as an
exasperated but very human and sensible drinker. More well
unified than his first satire, "Cauld Comfort" is one of the poet's
finest achievements.

Two weeks later, he wrote another poem that satirized the
temperance advocates, and it is also very successful. In "Huyler's
Ghost," the poet portrays himself as dozing before the fire one
night, in the back parlor of Jabez Capps' Grocery, when he is
suddenly confronted by the ghost of the town drunk. (Perhaps the
closest thing to this poem in American literature is Lowell's
"Su'thin' in the Line o' Pastoral" in *The Bigelow Papers,* but in that
work, it is the ghost of the poet's Puritan ancestor who appears.)
Much of the poem's value resides in the delightful comic charac-
terization of Old Huyler, who proceeds to demonstrate that his
addiction to whiskey has survived the grave. As he says at one
point, speaking with a Dutch accent, "'Whiskey's a gure for every
ill;/Libing or dead, I lub it still.'" Earlier in the poem, he makes a
colorful attack upon the temperance crusaders, whose severe
approach to their fellow men has made Springfield a "dismal"
town. In the prose preface to the lyric, the poet offers a sympathet-
ic description of Old Huyler, and the poem itself demonstrates
that he was, after all, a harmless, friendly fellow, more deserving of
laughter than reproach. In other words, H's decision to put
criticism of the temperance advocates into the mouth of a jovial
drunk was a masterstroke, for against Old Huyler their attitude of
moral severity would seem repressive, as well as useless.

"To the Small Beer Poets" and "The Remonstrance" deal with
women, bachelors, marriage, and related matters—sometimes
satirically and sometimes with genuine appreciation—as the poet
examines the pleasures, follies, and exasperations of love. The

former presents these topics as potential subject matter for the other local poets, whom H. liked to ridicule in print. The following passage, for example, displays this double focus of the poem (love and literature):

> When ma'am, trick'd out in silks and laces,
> Makes a thousand queer grimaces,
> Her head she tosses high in air—
> That makes the honest bumpkin stare—
> And cocks her nose up so together,
> Like pigs when they espy foul weather.
> This sets your poetasters mad,
> Who snort like calves that feel the gad;
> And mounted on their own tame jackus,
> Think all the while they stride Pegassus.
> 'Tis this inflicts the town with rhymes,
> (When bad, the worst of all bad crimes.)

While it has some fine passages, "To the Small Beer Poets" is not as well unified as the poet's best satires.

With regard to "The Remonstrance," seldom has love been viewed in such a well-rounded fashion within the confines of a lyric poem. After beginning with a forty-four-line reproof, supposedly from those who feel he should abandon satire for love poetry, H. defends himself. In the process, he criticizes the vanity of women, celebrates the joys of married life, analyzes love and courtship, and satirizes old bachelors like himself. Especially interesting is his portrait of the bachelor as a frustrated lover, whose mind produces visions as he sits alone by the fire (lines 133-68). "The Remonstrance" is a very entertaining poem, and at 238 lines, it is the poet's longest work.

Along with "To the Small Beer Poets," three other satires deal, in very different ways, with the writing of poetry by H. and his contemporaries in early Illinois: "To 'The Prairie Bard,'" "Bards and Reviewers," and "Lament for the Small Beer Poets." The first of these is a verse epistle in Scots, directed to a poet in nearby Jacksonville who signed his works (in the *Illinois Patriot*) with that pseudonym. H. probably did not know that The Prairie Bard was

John Howard Bryant, the youngest brother of William Cullen
Bryant, America's most celebrated poet of that era. In any case, he
recognized the man's poetic talent—which was second only to that
of H. in early Illinois—and he recommends in the poem that they
devote themselves to writing poetry about the West. In fact, he
closes by challenging The Prairie Bard to a poetry-writing contest,
with the rivers of their home counties (the Sangamon and the
Mauvaisterre) as subject matter. Bryant eventually responded
with a poem called "To H.," although he declared in it that the
Mauvaisterre was not worth celebrating.[12] If H. wrote a poem on
the Sangamon River, it has not survived.

But "To 'The Prairie Bard'" is not simply a serious poem, for
elsewhere in the 117-line lyric H. gently satirizes Jacksonville. It
was heavily influenced by New Englanders (unlike Springfield,
where emigrants from frontier states were just as influential as
easterners), and so it had a different moral climate, as the poet
indicates:

> They tell me, too, ye're unco civil,
> And do the gude—eschewing evil;
> That in your town nae man gets drunk,
> Nor can be found a single punk.
> Heigh, sirs, that I could say as much
> For Springfield, but I can't—in dutch!

The poet also mentions that he's heard of Jacksonville's "pin-
cushion society," and he asks that the ladies who organized it send
him one. Evidently one of them did so, for in August of that year he
published a brief poetic thank-you note entitled "On the Present
of a Pincushion by a Lady." In any case, although it is interesting,
"To 'The Prairie Bard'" is not one of the poet's finest satires.

"Bards and Reviewers" is also essentially a verse epistle, but it
is a much better poem. In fact, it is a superb defense of the poet's
commitment to writing poetry in and about the western frontier.
Early in 1832, a would-be critic in Jacksonville wrote a newspaper
article that criticized the Springfield poets (that is, those who were
publishing lyrics in the *Sangamo Journal*). The article does not
survive, but H. indicates that it was signed "Scrutator" (the one

who scrutinizes). In making his response, the poet produced his most complex satire. The opening is particularly effective, as H. reduces the critic's name to a comic clipped form (*"Scru"*) and then attacks the foundation of his criticism:

> *Scruter, Scrutator, Scru*—which is't
> That you subscribe your classic fist?
> I am not gifted sore with Latin,
> But one or t'other 'tis, that's sartin.
> *Poeta nascitur, non fit—*
> Poets are born, not made—that's it.
> This is the text from which you screw
> Your hypercriticism through,
> And to the modest bard dispense
> Your critic bile—a mere pretence.
> Horace should teach you better sense.

Since H. had already criticized the Springfield poets himself, he wrote "Bards and Reviewers" from the perspective of a "small beer poet"—rather than in his own voice. Hence, the speaker occasionally criticizes H. as well as Scrutator: "Why join with H., that renegado,/Who treats us like a Winnebago?" Later in the poem, the speaker defends the writing of poetry by those who do not possess real genius—and in the process, he makes a case for poetry that is not devoted to subjects of high seriousness. He says of the small-beer poets,

> Shakespeares, indeed, they may not be,
> But still, they're poets in degree.
> Milton's vast stores they don't possess,
> And yet, they may not please the less;
> Nor do pretend within their scope
> The ease and elegance of Pope.
> Is there in verse no medium found,
> But all must still be classic ground,
> Sublime, most elegant, profound?

And then, toward the end of the poem, when the speaker wants to recommend the writing of poetry about the West, he introduces H., who speaks in his own voice (Scots dialect) to poke fun at The Prairie Bard and claim for himself the title "Bard of Sangamo." Hence, "Bards and Reviewers" is sophisticated in its handling of poetic voice. As a defense of regional literature, it is likely to be viewed as one of the most important poems ever written about the early Midwest.

In "Lament for the Small Beer Poets" H. returns to his more familiar role as the chief critic of Springfield's rhymesters. He left town late in 1832, and by the time he came back early in 1833, the poetic activity that he had helped to promote had dissipated. This motivated H. to criticize the local poets for abandoning their craft:

> Say, hath Scrutator screw'd you down
> That you no more amuse the town;
> Veto'd the issue of your brains
> (The product of such mental pains,)
> That still would wriggle into life
> Like tadpoles when the Spring is rife?

This leads into a humorous description of the difficulties involved in writing poetry, especially for the frontier settler with family responsibilities.

Since the first half of the poem consists of three stanzas on the disappearance of the local poets, and the second half is a continuous verse paragraph on the problems that may beset a poet, it is likely that "Lament for the Small Beer Poets" was written in two parts, with the second being added as an afterthought. In spite of this, it is fairly well unified, and like most of the other satires, it is vigorously written and very entertaining.

The one remaining satire, "On the Arrival of the First Steam Boat," focuses on an event of great interest to residents of early Springfield. In March of 1832, a steamboat called the *Talisman* came up the Sangamon River as far as Springfield, and people there thought that its arrival signaled the start of economic prosperity for the town. But a couple of days later, the water level of the river—which had been abnormally high due to melting snow—began to fall, and the boat hurried away, never to return. The initial excitement of local residents, who celebrated the arrival in various ways, prompted H. to treat the event in mock-heroic style.

This is apparently the only poem by H. that has been noticed by scholars. Benjamin P. Thomas, in *Lincoln's New Salem* (1934), Paul M. Angle, in *"Here I Have Lived": A History of Lincoln's Springfield* (1935), and Edgar Lee Masters, in *The Sangamon* (1942), all quote lines from it when discussing the *Talisman* incident, but none of them comments on the poem, or refers to the initial H., or recognizes that the same poet wrote other lyrics as well.[13]

Undoubtedly, they were not aware of the mock-heroic technique of the poem and, hence, did not realize that it was a satire about, as well as a commemoration of, the steamboat's arrival. Yet this is apparent from the outset, as the poet compares the event to Jason's quest for the Golden Fleece and the discovery of America by Columbus—thus trivializing the local achievement by comparison. He later satirizes the townspeople for their overreaction, presenting them as frontier boobs who do not know what to make of a steamboat, although he also depicts himself as pleased with the venture and willing to commemorate it in verse:

> Our Bard, they say, e'en cock'd his eye,
> And seemed a moment to beguile
> His care-worn phiz into a smile;
> And when he could no longer doubt it,
> Made a bran' new song about it.

No other satire by H. so clearly reveals his position in Springfield as the much-admired "Bard of Sangamo"—at once the most penetrating critic and most staunch supporter of that frontier community.

Those lyrics which have been classified in this edition as Poems on Nature are chiefly descriptive, and they clearly display the poet's romantic sensibility. For in spite of his obvious debt to eighteenth-century satirical poetry, he was essentially a product of the Romantic Period, with its emphasis on the poet's emotions, response to wild nature, glorification of the commonplace, use of common language, poetic spontaneity, and philosophical nonconformity. "To the Frogs," for example, is a nature meditation similar to William Cullen Bryant's "The Prairies," and since the former appeared in 1838, it could have been inspired by that famous poem, published in 1833. However, the poet's meditation produces a vision of the recently vanished Indians of the Sangamon country rather than Bryant's prehistoric mound builders. Also of special interest is "Lines on the Approach of Winter." It includes a romantic description of winter's indoor pleasures (lines 29-44) that is similar to parts of Whittier's *Snow-Bound,* which appeared thirty-four years later. The lyric concludes with the poet focusing on an important concept of the Romantic Period, sympathy:

> Sweet power, that for another's woe
> Prompts the feeling tear to flow,
> May I ne'er shut my heart to thee,
> For what is life but sympathy?

In another fine poem, "The Approach of Spring," H. describes the midwestern countryside and village as effectively as any poet before the Chicago Renaissance. The lyric is especially interesting because the poet includes aspects of the season (mud, pigs) that would have been considered unpoetic by most people in his time, along with other manifestations (loafers, politicians) that are probably found in no other poem of the spring. However, it concludes with a couplet that depicts very conventional springtime behavior: "Sweet faces now are seen along the way;/The beaus are smart, and hens begin to lay." These lines effectively juxtapose human courtship and animal reproduction, thus suggesting that the same elemental forces of nature are responsible for both activities.

In contrast, several nature poems display the poet's recognition that the natural world in the West could be an inhospitable and even dangerous place, especially for the solitary traveler. For example, a poem called "Sonnet" ("Fierce overhead the fervid dog-star reigns") describes the hottest time of the summer, when "every living thing, by heat opprest,/Seeks some cool cover for a place of rest." Another lyric—and a better one—entitled "Winter," mentions traveling in "Cold chilling winds" and "drizzling rain." The latter ends with a serio-comic appeal to Christians to assist any traveler who comes to the door in such weather: "if the temperance pledge ye have not taken,/Give him a dram, a bed, and slice of bacon."

Even more significant is "Wolves," a powerful blank verse study of a winter traveler doomed to die in the snow-covered wasteland of the prairie:

> . . . down he sinks at last, and black despair
> Brings hideous shapes and fancies to his eyes.
> Meanwhile, faintly at first, and mingled with the blast,
> The long, loud howl of wolves upon his track
> Is now distinctly heard.

This poem is especially effective because H. does not actually describe the wolf attack but, rather, focuses on the growing terror of the traveler. Moreover, the winter weather itself is described with words like "fierce" and "savage," so that when the wolves finally appear, they simply embody the vicious antagonism of the season. In other words, "Wolves" challenges the prevailing romantic conception of a benign natural world. Furthermore, the poem closes with the winter moon shining "calm and cold upon the pallid scene" in spite of the traveler's appeal to heaven for help, which emphasizes that man is not the object of concern of a benevolent God. This view of man—struggling in a universe that is indifferent to his welfare—was, of course, unconventional in the early nineteenth century.

A couple of the most interesting nature poems are comic. "Vernal Musings" begins as a nature meditation, but when the poet's mind turns from "The prairie's wild and native son" (the Indian) to the pioneer culture in which he finds himself, his verse becomes humorous. Also, "Sonnet to the Frogs" is a unique item, not only because it is a comic sonnet, but because it has a lengthy and entertaining prose prologue in which the poet describes the circumstances that caused him to write the poem. It begins with a spring walk: "Tired with yawning over the fire in my little back parlor last Sunday—reading the productions of the small-beer poets and comparing one cat-muse with another—I wandered forth into the woods that so agreeably skirt our thriving little town, and while contrasting in my mind the pleasant aspect they presented last summer with their present desolate appearance, I was glad to hear again the cheerful notes of the frogs. . . ." And it ends with the poet sitting on a stump, playing his jew's harp, and warning the frog-singers to beware of "critics in the neighbor town," especially "the Scru" (Scrutator). The preface and sonnet together offer an entertaining depiction of a romantic poet—albeit one with a humorous inclination—in the act of composing a lyric.

The section labelled Short Philosophical Lyrics includes poems that are essentially analytical rather than descriptive, although a few also reflect the natural world. The most common theme is death, which may have been promoted by H's reading of the Graveyard Poets, who were popular during his youth in the late eighteenth and early nineteenth centuries. In fact, one of his poems is entitled "Written Near Springfield Church-yard" and is a meditation on the dead who lie in that village cemetery. But while the Graveyard Poets were essentially confident of man's immortality, in spite of their expression of melancholy, H. always views death with great apprehension because he lacks that certitude. Hence, the closing lines of the poem emphasize that the dead are forever removed from the joys of life—and also imply that there is no evidence of a resurrection:

> Yet so it is—the dead return no more.
> Forever silent, here they still remain.
> No wandering ghost from Pluto's gloomy shore
> Ever returned to say, "we come again."

This thematic stress on death is another link between H. and William Cullen Bryant, who was also influenced by the Graveyard Poets.

One of the Springfield poet's most effective lyrics on death is "Spirits," a sonnet which closes with the following sestet:

They say, at certain times, without control,
The buried dead at this dark watch appear;
A sudden horror tells their presence near,
With shrieks upon the gale that chill the soul—
Such was the sound which late the night winds bore,
Like some poor wretch thrown bleeding on the shore.

The closing image very effectively objectifies the poet's feeling of "sudden horror," mentioned a few lines earlier. This lyric goes beyond mere uncertainty about man's existence after death to present H's deep fear that death may be perpetual anguish.

In one of his other sonnets ("This vapor we call life is but a breath,"), the poet considers the significance of death. After he realizes that the inquiring mind can learn nothing, he concludes, "Dim mists, and dark impenetrable gloom/For ever shroud this secret of the tomb." That this uncertainty about death caused the poet to doubt the truth of Christianity is evident from a poem entitled "L'envoy," which appeared with the above-mentioned sonnet and was probably intended as a companion piece. The darkness mentioned at the end of the sonnet becomes metaphorical, in "L'envoy," for the poet's mental condition. The latter poem places him in a symbolic landscape where a shepherd and a star point the way out of a dark wood (named Error), thus implying that Christian belief offers guidance for those who are in a mental or spiritual quandary. The shepherd also explains that reason alone can not provide the answers to some questions. However, the poem does not close with H. setting off in the recommended direction, so while he recognized that his speculations about death offered no illumination, Christian belief may have been—to use Frost's phrase—"the road not taken."

That the poet realized there was a deep conflict between faith and reason—or Christianity and the Enlightenment, in cultural terms—is also apparent from a sonnet entitled "The Improvement of Modern Times":

Now, for a thousand years, the world has lain
In deepest ignorance and mental night;
At length breaks forth the cheerful light,

And mind resumes her long disputed reign.
Fell superstition, by the vapors fed,
Engender'd in the dark abyss of time;
The morning sun far hence hath sped,
And Science takes her onward march sublime.
The dreams of ignorance no more prevail;
The monk is gone, the convent low is laid,
And all their nonsense but the idle tale
Of some old crone still ling'ring in the shade.
The nations now a brighter vigil keep,
And stand erect, like giants rous'd from sleep.

H. makes greater use of imagery here than in most of his other
sonnets. Of course, the main image is that of mankind arising from
a long sleep in the dark, and the sun is a natural symbol of the
Enlightenment that rouses man (or the nations of the world) from
that "mental night" where "dreams of ignorance" prevail. It is
interesting to note that, in the third quatrain, the poet clearly
blames Christianity for keeping man in the darkness. Hence, this
poem contrasts sharply with "L'envoy," where Christianity is
presented as a light in the dark wood of Error.

Two other lyrics that express a contrast which is indicative of
the poet's philosophical uncertainty are "Sonnet" ("Though in a
wayward mood, at times I stray") and "Astrology Fallacious." In
the former, the speaker takes notice of the stars and wonders,
"Shall he, when life's poor fluttering dream is past,/Range their
bright field and rest in heav'n at last?" In the other poem, H. views
the night sky as a beautiful phenomenon but certainly not
indicative of a spiritual home for man. Indeed, he depicts the
heavens as lovely but otherwise unrelated to human life—and thus
implies that the universe is indifferent to man's welfare.

Among the other Short Philosophical Lyrics are two fine
sonnets in which the poet deals with intellectual development.
Both of them are simply entitled "Sonnet." The one displays a
remarkable dynamism in the first and second quatrains, as the
speaker considers the result of his efforts to realize his deepest
hopes:

How like myself in former years and now;
Yet how unlike, my fortune still the same.
The scene alone is chang'd; still on my brow
Rests the dead calm that hides a soul all flame.
Musing, yet restless; thoughtful, yet not wise;
Ling'ring, yet onward still, my steps pursue
A phantom shapeless, that deludes these eyes,
Which if I follow not doth still pursue.

This sonnet is especially effective because it reveals the self in conflict. Had H. written more like it, his achievement in the sonnet might have been very significant indeed. The poem ends with the speaker admitting that his pursuit of self-fulfillment has unfortunately led him "To gather thorns where I expected flowers,/And in life's lowest scene consume the hours."

The other sonnet depicts life as a ceaseless struggle and considers the relationship between maturity and perception:

To struggle on, to struggle on for aye—
This seems of man th' inexorable doom.
And yet how quickly glides his life away—
No rest between the cradle and the tomb.
In youth, too eager and with spirits light,
We still anticipate a brighter sphere,
Filling the mind with fancies all too bright,
And revel in the visions insincere.
Yet in the real can only truth be found.
When sad experience lifts the veil between,
No longer then we tread on fairy ground,
But view with sober eye the common scene:
Plain truth alone and unadorned we see,
Life's vulgar prose and stern reality.

The remarkable rhythmic variation of the poem both emphasizes the individual lines and contributes to the powerful close. Like most of the poet's sonnets, it is virtually devoid of metaphor—the sole exception being the phrase "Life's vulgar prose" in the final line. However, the lack of metaphor is particularly appropriate in this sonnet, since the very subject of the poem is the "stern reality"—unmitigated by imaginative vision—which eventually confronts all men.

There are only three works in the section of this edition called Poems on Legend and Mythology, but they are among the most distinctive and interesting items in H's canon. In "Taur Arthur" the poet meditates on a rock along the coast of Cornwall not far from where he was raised, and the associations between himself and that place are revealed to be both personal and cultural. At the outset, the poet contrasts his present circumstances in America with his younger days in Cornwall. Spring comes to the frontier, but for him "all is sad and wild and lone,/Like winter near the old grey stone." In other words, he feels out of tune with the spring, for he is overcome by a sense of isolation from his homeland. (The same notion is also expressed in "When Will the Spring Return?," lines 29-32, but in that lyric H. attempts no poetic rapprochement with his native country, as he does in "Taur Arthur.") He then recalls being with his beloved Lela on the coast of Cornwall, and that leads into a meditation about the historic region he came from, "Where still the sons of Arthur keep,/And where they still defy the deep." In the climactic section of the poem (lines 48-76), he celebrates the heritage of Cornwall—and his own heritage as a poet—through the use of Arthurian folklore from that area. Thoroughly British in inspiration, "Taur Arthur" is a haunting blend of personal reminiscence and Cornish legend.

"The Hall of Odin" focuses on comradeship and conflict in Valhalla, as it examines the role of poetry in medieval Scandanavian culture. *The Poetic Edda* had a direct influence on the poem, and numerous explanatory footnotes—the only ones provided by H. for any of his works—reveal that the poet's study of Norse mythology was considerable. Included in the poem is a lengthy summary of a few stories from that mythology (as told by a singer of tales), which concludes with a brief account of "the twilight of the gods" (lines 69-80). This is preceded by a summary of "The Lay of Thrym" (about the regaining of Thor's hammer), as if to suggest that conflict, such as depicted in that famous story, will promote the coming of "that fatal day/When all the gods must pass away." Also, "The Lay of Thrym" was probably intended to warn the listening warriors of Lok's (Loki's) treachery, since his deception made possible the destruction of the giants by Thor.

H. attempts to show that poetry was essential to the continuation of society in Old Norse culture, for as soon as the warriors in Valhalla fail to heed the cultural message of the scald, a battle erupts, induced by Lok. It is stopped only when the voice of Odin (who dispenses the gift of poetry, according to H.) thunders across the battlefield. Odin evidently represents societal order—in the poet's view—and so when his consort (here named Freia) appears at the end of the poem, she embodies a quality that thrives only in an ordered society: love. The closing couplet emphasizes the impact of that quality on the warriors of Valhalla—and implies the temporary cessation of their drift toward societal destruction: "She moves a queen in Odin's hall,/And leads each captive heart in thrall."

Without a doubt, "The Hall of Odin" was an attempt by H. to write a poem of elevated subject matter and style, not to mention serious meaning. Although it is not a brilliant achievement, the narrative has many powerful lines and considerable complexity. Moreover, it is a very successful portrayal of heroic culture, which makes "The Hall of Odin" a rare item in British poetry of the nineteenth century and unique in the American tradition.

The third poem in the Legend and Mythology group, "The Gods of Old," is not as important as either of the others, but part of it relates closely to the subject matter of "The Hall of Odin." Like that poem and "Taur Arthur," it focuses on the role of the poet in earlier cultures. In "The Gods of Old," however, H. indicates that very early poets were the creators of the gods, and hence were deserving of an exalted social positon. In contrast, modern poets—living in an age of less imagination, perhaps—are often disregarded:

> But in these vile degenerate days
> There's few that give the poet praise,
> While each dull knave in duller prose can shine,
> And cant and nonsense now are hail'd divine.

Poems on Transience and Remembrance contains fourteen items, none of which is among H's finest achievements. Although those lyrics are generally conventional in subject matter, the poet's facility often makes them well worth reading, as illustrated by these lines from "A Sonnet":

> And what is life, that we so fondly crave?
> In youth a torment—curse in after years—
> A path that leads forever to the grave,
> Whether in joy pursued, or else in tears. . . .

Another short lyric, entitled "Many Years Ago," has ballad-like simplicity and repetition, which make it fairly effective. But perhaps the best poem in this group is "Secret Sorrow," in which the theme of remembrance quickly leads into a more promising topic, as the poet reflects on his characteristic concealment of his true feelings:

> Then deem not, though I seem so gay,
> Without a latent trace of ill,
> For mostly then my looks betray—
> When gayest I am saddest still.
>
> The cause of this is easy shown:
> We would not that our thoughts be known.
> Experience teaches us, and pride,
> The sorrows of the heart to hide.

Three lyrics entitled "Lines" find the poet attempting to deal with the problem of transience, which was a major concern for him—as it was for his contemporary, Bryant. The first ("Dark o'er my brow the vanished years") is simply an illustration of the notion that memory can "for a while the past renew," as the poet recalls being with his beloved near the Thames River. The second ("When I recall the days gone by,") asserts that since transience is inevitable, the individual should focus on the joys of the present. H. views the medieval Persian poet, Hafez of Shiraz, who often celebrated the satisfactions of life, as a model for himself to

emulate. The third poem ("How speed our lives away—") sets
forth a philosophical solution to the problem: the individual dies
but the forms of nature remain. Thus, as long as mankind
continues, the gifts of nature will be his to enjoy. While these
poems are not fine achievements, they do reveal that the poet was
not content to simply assert the stock Christian response to
transience: that it is unimportant because man is destined .to
reside with God.

Included in this section are a few lyrics in which H. longs to be in
England again. Since they were written over a number of years
(1833, 1838, 1845), it is evident that he did not return to his native
land during that period. In fact, a brief poem entitled "The Wish"
reveals the poet's desire to be buried in England, as if to suggest
that returning before his death could not be considered. The title
of another poem, "The Exile," also suggests that H. felt compelled
to remain abroad, although the lyric itself does not explicitly
convey that idea.

Both of the poems in the section called Two Lyrics on the Black
Hawk War are of little value. The first, "On the Second Arming
against Black Hawk," is an attempt to celebrate the conflict
between Indians and soldiers that many pioneers felt was coming
in the spring of 1832. As H. says at one point, "mixed with shouts,
and savage screams,/The combat thickens in my dreams." But the
lyric also changes after line eighty-five, and the final forty-four
lines are a comic self-portrait in which the poet (referring to
himself in the third person) describes his aversion to battle:

> Then do not drag him to the wars;
> No taste has he for wounds and scars.
> He spills no blood, but only ink,
> And at the scalping knife would blink.
> But though the Bard himself is tame,
> He measures out the hero's fame. . . .

During August of that year, H. had the opportunity to measure out
a hero's fame by praising James D. Henry's role in that frontier
conflict—which had by then come to an end. Henry was a general
in the Illinois militia, and he lived in Springfield. The poet was

probably encouraged to compose a lyric about him by some of the many local residents who ardently supported the militia's participation in the war. He left the poem untitled, which may be an indication that he had little interest in praising heroes after all.

The final section of this edition, Miscellaneous Short Lyrics, includes five items which do not fit into the other categories. None is among H's best poems, although the three comic pieces are worth reading. "On the Present of a Pincushion by a Lady" is a humorous verse letter in Scots, in which the poet thanks an admirer for a small gift. Although trivial in subject matter, the lyric displays the kind of vitality found in H's satires and, thus, is fairly effective. "L'amour Coquet" is a comic pastoral narrative about a maiden who loses her beloved. The poet makes fun of the common pastoral values of innocence and fidelity. "The Independent Philosopher" is not really a philosophical poem but a brief comic assertion that the poet intends to call it "quits" with the world and go his own way. The two serious lyrics, "Il Melancolico per Amore" and "Sonnet" ("There is a charm in foreign lands to be,"), contain recollections of H's visits to Italy and Spain.

Considering the relatively small size of his canon—ninety-three items—H. has an unusual number of fine poems to his credit. "Hame's the Best Place A'ter A'," "Cauld Comfort," "Huyler's Ghost," "Bards and Reviewers," "The Remonstrance," "Lament for the Small Beer Poets," "To the Frogs," "The Approach of Spring," "Winter," "Wolves," "Astrology Fallacious," "Taur Arthur," "The Hall of Odin," and several very effective sonnets add up to a significant literary achievement.

Unlike other midwestern poets of the earlier nineteenth century —such as James Hall, Otway Curry, and William D. Gallagher—H. can stand to be compared with the finest eastern poets of that era, especially Bryant, Whittier, Longfellow, and Lowell. (This is not to say that his achievement equals theirs, but that he was a poet of similar capability.) Like them, he used conventional poetic forms and easily comprehensible language. Hence, he did not develop a kind of poetry that was unique, or indigenous to the West. However, he did emphasize the importance of western subject matter in "To 'The Prairie Bard'" and "Bards and Reviewers," and he wrote a number of satires, nature poems, and sonnets that reflected the West more effectively than any other poems of his era. Thus, like New England's Fireside Poets, he should perhaps be classified as a sectionalist. And there are many other similarities between H. and those famous literary figures: like Bryant, he frequently wrote about nature, mutability, and death; like Whittier, he was greatly influenced by Burns, and he had a tendency to idealize the past; like Longfellow, he had an interest in medieval Scandanavian culture, and he was an effective sonneteer; and like Lowell, he was a satirist who wrote vigorous poetic lines and occasionally created interesting speakers for his poems. It is also worth noting that H's debt to the Graveyard School of Poetry, emphasis on transience, interest in satire, use of the closed couplet, and humanitarian concern make him akin to Philip Freneau. However, the latter was predominantly influenced by neo-classical thought and writing, while H. was essentially a romantic poet.

Like all five of the writers mentioned above, H. was often not probing or subtle enough to be thought-provoking, and his poems lack originality of technique and metaphoric complexity. On the other hand, in his satires he wrote some of the most vigorous and imaginative poetry yet to appear in America; in his finest nature poems he achieved a remarkable smoothness without sacrificing vitality of expression; in lyrics like "Wolves" and "Astrology Fallacious" he challenged the prevailing conception of a benign, man-centered universe; in his best sonnets he examined the most disturbing aspects of his inner life and often powerfully expressed his realizations; in "Taur Arthur" he created a successful meditative poem about his Cornish heritage, and in "The Hall of Odin" he produced a stirring and significant portrayal of heroic culture. Hence, the range of his poetic capability was considerable, and his achievement is large enough to warrant a modern readership. Considered as a British author, H. is simply a talented minor poet of the Romantic Period—distinguished chiefly for his focus on the American frontier, his humor, and his facility as both a satirist and sonneteer. On the other hand, viewed as part of the American tradition, he is the finest poet of his era in the Midwest.

Notes to the Introduction

[1]*Sangamo Journal,* 10 May, 1832, p.1.

[2]*The Literary Gazette,* 4 (1818), 527, 624, 720.

[3]*The Literary Gazette,* 9 (1821), 75. See also the review of John Hartnoll's first poem (which appeared as a brief book) in the *Gazette,* 9 (1821), 69.

[4]"Springfield," *Sangamo Journal,* 19 Jan., 1832, p. 3.

[5]Untitled Poem, *Sangamo Journal,* 9 Feb., 1832, p. 3.

[6]"To H.," *Sangamo Journal,* 24 May, 1832, p. 4.

[7]"To H.," *Sangamo Journal,* 31 May, 1832, p. 2.

[8]*Letters from Illinois* (Philadelphia: M. Carey and Son, 1818), p. 19. Birkbeck wrote to a friend that "England was never so dear to me as it is now in the recollection," and yet he declared that America was "a land of Liberty" while his native country was not (p. 19). Thus, his situation was probably very similar to the poet's.

[9]Scholarship on this subject does exist, but it is very limited. The two most important studies of early midwestern literature do not mention any poetry of significance from that period: Dorothy Anne Dondore, *The Prairie and the Making of Middle America* (1926; rpt. New York: Antiquarian Press, 1961), pp, 239-70; Ralph Leslie Rusk, "Poetry," *The Literature of the Middle Western Frontier* (New York: Columbia Univ. Press, 1925), I, 303-51. Two recent articles on the subject also do not refer to poetry of genuine value from the early Midwest: Bernard F. Engel, "Poetry of the Early Midwest," *Midwestern Miscellany,* 6 (1978), 21-29; John T. Flanagan, "Poetic Voices in the Early Middle West," *The Centennial Review,* 24 (1980), 269-83.

[10]"Lines on the Mounds in the Cahokia Prairie, Illinois," in Timothy Flint, *Recollections of the Last Ten Years in the Valley of the Mississippi* (Boston: Cummings, Hilliard, 1826), pp. 167-68.

11"The Prairie," *Illinois Monthly Magazine,* 1 (1831), 570-71.

12See "To H.—1831," *The Life and Poems of John Howard Bryant* (Elmwood, Illinois: [no publisher], 1894), pp. 105-08. When the poem was first published—in the *Illinois Patriot* and *Sangamo Journal*—it was simply entitled "To H." See note seven above.

13Benjamin P. Thomas, *Lincoln's New Salem* (1934; rpt. Chicago: Lincoln's New Salem Enterprises, 1973), p. 76; Paul M. Angle, *"Here I Have Lived": A History of Lincoln's Springfield* (Springfield: The Abraham Lincoln Association, 1935), pp. 37-38; Edgar Lee Masters, *The Sangamon* (New York: Farrar and Rinehart, 1942), p. 174. Probably all three of these authors ran across the passage from "On the Arrival of the First Steam Boat" that is quoted in the *History of Sangamon County* (Chicago: Inter-state Publishing Co., 1881), p. 53—and so they may have never read the satire in its entirety. The 1881 volume also says nothing about the poem or the poet.

Early Poems

1

Sonnet:
After the Ancient Style

This little booke the gentle muse hath penn'd
When that she had an idle hour to lose,
What time the evening shades do broad extend,
Or sheeny morn walks forth among the dews.
And shouldst thou, goodman reader, there espy
Somewhat ungainsome in the muse's style,
Do not, for that, her work fling careless by—
It may ygret the ingle-nook awhile.
And think thee, critic of a brow malign,
Whose up-turn'd nose declares your cank'ring spite,　　10
That ye mote not offend the sacred nine,
Ne censure what thou canst not set aright.
Go forth, then, little booke, and speed thee fair,
For well I wot thou hast my special pray'r.

2

Sonnet:
To My Lamp

So sweetly calm thy soft light spreadeth here,
Where I now sit enjoying Fancy's dreams,
That I could grieve, the morning drawing near,
So soon to lose thy clear and yellow beams.
To me thou seemest like the studious mind,
Whose tranquil flame a genial spirit tends,
Which as it brighter grows and more refined,
The sooner, then, its fragile being ends.
Fair light! thy modest radiance wins my heart,
And it is joy alone to gaze on thee.   10
I care not for the day; let it depart,
Beneath thy gentle influence still to be.
More pleasing far the hour of midnight deep,
To watch thy rays when all the world's asleep.

3

Sonnet

Noire filles de nuit, douces et cheres ombres,
Je cherche un sur azile en vos retraites sombres.
Deshoulieres

I seek the dark and lone retreat,
Unknown, untrod by human feet,
The [fens] by day, the woods by night,
And love those scenes which men affright.
When Spring appear'd in all her charms,
I felt the pow'r of love's soft arms;
But with stern Winter's frown there came
Not hope—despair, not love—disdain.
Since then, all joys from me are fled.
The mansions of the silent dead   10
I'll seek—there make my nightly moan
To all, save night's dull bird, unknown,
For o'er this sad and stricken heart
Despair hath fixed her keenest dart.

4

Sonnet

I seek the fields, the woods, and gentle streams,
In hopes to pass some calm refreshing hours;
But ah! how weak are all my idle dreams—
Love, love alone my bleeding heart devours.
Or if mine eye a glance of pleasure shew
On some sweet object—hill or circling plain—
Quick comes the thought that causes all my woe,
My spirits sink, and I am sad again.
For since that beauteous and all-lovely fair
Hath from these arms by saddest fate been torn,   10
Her dear rememb'rance is my only care,
And for her sake alone I weep and mourn!
But vain are tears by fondest friendship shed,
Nor sighs or tears can animate the dead.

5

Sonnet

Solo e pensoso i piu deserti campi,
Vo misurando a passi tardi e lenti.

These days of mis'ry, loved one, for thy sake
My feeble frame were well content to bear—
But when I think that thou too dost partake
Of sorrow's bitter pang and hast of grief thy share,
O then my fainting heart no refuge finds,
And darkest thoughts fill my lorn soul with woe.
At night, when all is hush'd, save the rude winds,
I pass like [a] spectre forth, unweeting where I go.
How changed the scene, alas! when hope's gay dream
Bade me to think that every joy was near.   10
Now I, awaking, like a lost one seem,
And find on either side th' prospect sad and drear.
Thus mournfully away each day doth glide,
Consumed with aching cares and grief's o'erwhelming tide.

6

Sonnet:
To Melancholy

Pale blue-eye'd maid! that ever lov'st to rove
Where the brown heath its darkest shadows throws,
Near lonely halls, or woods, or pensive grove,
And with th' ill-omen'd bird indulge thy woes;
Thee once I shunn'd, whilst life was young and new,
And all thy dreary haunts pass'd heedful by,
More pleas'd at early morn to brush the dew
Than with the evening gales to hear thee sigh.
But now thy glens and desert fens no more
Inspire a terror in my anxious heart;   10
Now I can wander by the sea-beat shore,
Nor feel a wish from the wild waves to part—
Though oft as I go forth in gloom and care,
I meet that wizard, dark and fell Despair!

7

Sonnet

Sweet Spring, thou com'st, but ah! my pleasant hours
And happy days with thee come not again.
Drummond

Now through the air the western breezes play,
And peeping buds put forth their callow heads;
The earth seems happy, and the new-born day,
Exulting, smiles o'er all the hills and meads.
That modest flower, attendant on the spring,
In many a hidden vale and silent wood,
In lovely bands greets him that's wandering,
And pleasantly relieves his thoughtful mood.
I, lone and pensive, bent by fortune low,
In this sweet season only live to weep.   10
And happy am I, if my stubborn wo
Yield a short respite in the arms of sleep—
But, then, I wake, and to my aching sight
The morning comes, to me a gloomier night.

8

Sonnet

i grati zefiri di primavera.
Metast.

Sweet Spring, thy young and soft love-beaming eye
Doth woo the tender buds to trust the day,
Whilst far from thee the angry gales do fly,
And genial showers thy welcome call obey.
Content, and joy, and pleasure's lovely train
Appear propitious with the light-wing'd hours,
And as they glide with rapture o'er the plain,
The zephyrs gently wake the early flowers.
At thy approach the weary fields rejoice,
And gladly reassume their native green;   10
All nature hears thy universal voice,
And feels thy influence through each varied scene.
Gay blooming maid, thy virgin sweets diffuse
A tranquil joy, that cheers the drooping muse.

9

Sonnet

Chiare, fresche e dolci acque.

Whilst that I wander in the pleasant fields,
Where lingers spring, enamour'd of their green,
A secret charm each lovely object yields,
Till even throws her dusky veil between.
And when at length the sullen shades prevail,
And night in sable clouds adown descends,
The modest moon emits a lustre pale
And to the meads her virgin beauty lends.
Then softer scenes and chaster thoughts arise,
As o'er the varied landscape stretching wide   10
The timid zephyr steals with sweet surprise,
And gently breathes upon the rippling tide,
Whose murmurs, softly pleasing to the ear,
Invite me to repose its green banks near.

10

Sonnet:
Written on Good Friday

The morning's breath, in meekness to the day,
Breathes o'er the fields a holy silence sweet,
Whilst the young flowers their tender buds display,
That pensive seem the hallowed morn to greet.
The sunny clouds swim lightly through the sky,
Tho' ting'd in parts with many a sombre hue;
Like hovering Fate on wings of Destiny,
Their course right on the heavenly road pursue.
And such a morn (more bright perchance) arose
When He, the Lamb of God, our Saviour, died;   10
What woe, what pain, he felt before the close
Of that sad day, on earth's yet to be tried.
O, Christians, mourn your Lord, him ceaseless bless,
Who for your good endured such deep distress.

11

Sonnet:
Winter

In these sad days, when cold and rain prevail,
I rest at home before a cheerful fire,
And with a book—perchance some olden tale
Of knights and arms—from all the world retire.
Beside me lie the cates upon the hearth,
While minstrel crickets tune a merry lay.
One little dog I have, and the whole earth
Can't shew a creature faithfuller than Tray.
What joy is mine! the wint'ry blast in vain
Against my cottage spends its idle rage,   10
And whilst rude floods oppress the neighb'ring plain,
I reckless sit, intent upon the page.
And sure, if mortal pleasure aught there be,
'Tis thus, to cheat the hours right pleasantly.

12

Sonnet:
The Poet Praises His Cat, Scracco

'Tis now six months and more, my whisker'd friend,
Since first thou peep'd within this narrow room,
The gift of one who did thy worth commend
And, thus, preserv'd thee from thy brother's doom.
Thou wast a kitten then, and gay of mind;
With thine own tail wouldst innocently play—
Most strangely puzzled that that thing behind
Should still escape, turn thee whichever way.
But now thou'rt grown a good and shapely cat,
Of aspect sage, that's seldom stirr'd with ire,   10
And though, indeed, thou art not very fat,
Thou sit'st content before my little fire—
Or, purring glad when spread our humble fare,
With gentle paw entreat'st thy slender share.

13

Sonnet:
The Poet Laments the Death
of His Cat, Scracco

Erewhile I did a gentle sonnet write
In praise of Scracco, my poor harmless cat,
And shew'd how many virtues could unite
In creatures that destroy the felon rat.
But she no more will doze before the fire,
And with grave luxury enjoy the heat,
Nor when from bus'ness dull I late retire,
Her weary master in strange antics greet.
The prowling rat no more will be her care,
Nor mouse, with aspect grim, to fright away.   10
These, now secure, purloin the mouldy fare,
And every dainty from the shelf convey.
Not so when my poor Scracco was alive,
For she far off the plundering herd would drive.

14

Sonnet

Le chat dort, e la nuit s'approche.

I will not hurt thee, sleek and gentle mouse,
Although you nib my cheese and spoil my bread.
No cat have I to scare thee from the house,
For she, alas! poor Scracco, now is dead.
Then fly not, little prowler, but remain,
And take the bits which from my table fall.
You're very welcome, nor will I complain
If, in a hungry fit, you eat up all.
Think not that Jemmy will thy life destroy;
(Jemmy is he who wears the scowling brow.)   10
His look, indeed, is stern, but then, my boy,
His heart's not wholly flint, I do avow.
So eat, and stuff thy little jacket well;
Feasts do not often come, that I can tell.

15

Sonnet:
To a Young Lady Musing

Thy face looks sad, fair maid, and yet that look
So sweetly doth become thy virgin brow
That one might soothly say he had mistook,
And gazed upon an angel here below.
Is it fond love which gives that tender shade
And casteth such soft witchery around?
Sure, love can never grieve so fair a maid,
And grief, though cruel, thee could never wound.
Perhaps thy soul, all tranquil and serene,
In meditation seeks its native sky,   10
And whilst it soars beyond this lowly scene,
Imparts that gentle sorrow to thine eye;
But whether love, or thought alone, it be,
It sheds a grace o'er maiden modesty.

16

Sonnet

Piu lune gia quand' i' feci 'l mal sonno,
Che del futuro mi squarcio 'l velame.

Whilst on the couch of pain and sorrow laid,
Mourning the past, that ne'er can be recall'd,
I cast my eyes toward the opening shade
Of future years—and start, at once appall'd.
There shadows direful and dim shapes appear,
Emerging slowly from the spectral gloom;
Disease, and pale remorse, love, hate, and fear
Are seen to drag their victim to the tomb.
The blighted buds of youth that promis'd fair—
Scath'd by the light'ning and the blasts of life—   10
Bright hopes and fond desires, lie scatter'd there,
The mock and scorn of all these forms of strife.
Thus, in the soul's dark twilight, I behold
That deadly vale, by many a dream foretold.

17

Sonnet

Thus rolls the restless world beneath the moon.
Drummond

Vain thoughts, vain hopes, and fond desires are fled,
Which early flutter'd round my infant heart.
And like fell dews their baneful influence shed—
More poisonous still when least we feel their smart.
My youth—a dream, a fleeting cloud—is gone,
Like that which passeth o'er a summer's day,
Or this, when night recedes from opening morn
And with it bears the vapour false away.
But what is now the waking dream I find?
Life's dull reality and sickly scene.   10
Alas! if we but knew for what we pined,
Scant our desires for such a world, I ween—
A world? a joyless waste where wretches weep,
And pain and sorrow their black vigils keep.

18

Sonnet

And King's Bench Walk by pleaders vocal made.
Anstey

There came to me a poor and care-worn clerk,
With visage thin and coat of rusty hue,
Who, with a sigh, did feelingly remark
The paucity of suits, and fees so few.
Just then the solemn clock slow tolled nine—
That fretful hour when clerks begin to wake,
And heavy with small beer (which they call wine)
Their way to Lincoln dull, or Gray's Inn pleasant take.
But he was of the Temple, which I think
The pleasantest of all the seats of law,   10
Nor less because 'tis near the river's brink
And not exactly in the city's maw.
But now, alas! few charms hath it to please
Sith there I draw out rhymes, where erst I drew out pleas.

19

Culloden

The wind blows loud,
The wind blows loud,
From off the wild and foaming water;
   But louder is the storm that pours
O'er Culloden's red field of slaughter.
   There swords have met—the bayonet
   And deadly dirk in blood are set,
   While gory streams the heath imbue—
   That morning only wet with dew.
   'Tis there the might of Caledon   10
   Fades before the stronger one—
   And the bleak sky looks coldly down
   On him who dared to reach a crown.
   The Saxon fiercely bears away
   The fortune of that hapless day,
   And man and babe and woman fall,
   Till one wide ruin covers all.

The wind blows loud,
The wind blows loud,
From off the wild and foaming water;   20
   But now no more the battle lours
O'er Culloden's dark field of slaughter.
   The trav'ller wand'ring there alone
   Hears but the night-wind's moan,
   And sometimes in a lonely bield
   Beholds the antique sword and shield.
   The pale moon rises o'er the scene
   As if no battle there had been—
   And the grey morn peeps gaily forth
   Where sleep the bravest of the North.   30

20

The Spectre

When night her solemn shadow throws
    Across the earth, I sink to rest,
And waking from a short repose,
    I mourn thee, absent from my breast.

And as the night-wind passeth by,
    Methinks I see thy pensive shade!
Methinks I hear a tender sigh
    The stillness of the hour invade.

"But why art thou so cold, my love,
    Thy full blue eye so fix'd and sad?   10
'Tis strange at this dark hour to rove,
    But stranger still the way thou'rt clad."

"I come from where no cares intrude,
    No levin blast is heard to blow,
Where silence reigns, and solitude
    Sits musing o'er the dead below.

And I have left that place of rest,
    And broke the fetters of the tomb,
Once more to slumber on thy breast,
    Then hie me to my lowly doom."   20

Why doth he start with wild affright?
    What means that horrid image there?
A grisly phantom blasts his sight,
    And down he sinks in black despair.

It is not she he loves so true,
    Sylvia, that young and blooming maid,
But one that sleeps beneath the yew,
    Whom he, the false one, has betray'd.

And thus she haunts his nightly dreams,
    Assuming that fair maiden's charms;   30
In vain he struggles—madly screams—
    A skeleton's within his arms.

21

Hodge

The wild winds blow,
Fast falls the snow,
And Nature looketh drear.
The fields and trees
The shepherd sees
Deck'd in their wintry gear.

The gobbling ducks,
The hen that clucks,
And cock that struts so bold,
The lowing cows,   10
And bleating ewes
Seem pinched by the cold.

The toiling steed
Regrets the mead
Where he was wont to browse.
The lazy hog
Grunts at the dog
That keeps him from the house.

But Grey-malkin,
All snug within,   20
Enjoys the blazing fire,
And sleek and fat,
Doth gently pat
The mouse that dares her ire.

Now Hodge returns!
The faggot burns,
The sparkling ale goes round;
The brown nuts too
Appear in view,
And mirth and glee abound.   30

The rosy maid,
Of man afraid,
Refuses to be kist;
And matrons grey
Fling care away
To play at loo and whist.

Such are the joys;
No care annoys
The happy countryman;
The winter howls,   40
The north wind scowls—
Hodge higher fills his can!

He heedeth not
The storm a jot,
Whilst all around is warm.
The hail may fall,
The wind may bawl;
These give him no alarm.

His barton's full.
The cow and bull   50
Shew Hodge's thrifty care;
And more than this,
His men, I wiss,
The farmer's kindness share.

No churl is he,
But blythe and free—
He bears a gen'rous heart;
And those that are
In fortune spare
Acknowledge his desert.   60

Now I will show
What mickle woe
Attends a town-led life,
And eke repeat
What seemeth meet,
Or single or with wife.

The air is thick,
The mud doth stick
And clog up all the way.
The busy crowd,   70
So dull and proud,
Wear out the dingy day.

At night they roam,
Are seldom home,
But in the tavern seen.
With throat like drum
His wife doth come,
A bitter shrew and quean.

"What, at your pot,
You lazy sot!"   80
She says in frantic fret;
But she, poor thing,
Gets a drubbing,
Which sure none can regret.

The single man
Looks pale and wan,
Th' effect of early riot.
It moves my ruth
To see the youth
So lost to health and quiet.   90

For ere he be
Full six times three,
By vile debauch he's undone,

And friends lament
In discontent
The wickedness of London.

The maidens flaunt
And gallivant,
Bedizen'd out so fine.
To church they run,   100
But never one
To list to the divine.

'Tis but to see
A certain he—
To plan how to deceive.
Miss, pert and vain,
Looks with disdain
On those that love believe.

In each new face
She finds a grace   110
Which her old lovers lack;
And then, God wot,
She heedeth not,
But stuns ye with her clack.

Thus have I shown
That in the town
The people do not well;
But honest Hodge
Doth fortune dodge
And gives and lives himsel'.   120

His ruddy cheek
And pimply beak
Shew little want or care.
He's early up,
Then takes a cup
And wends to field or fair.

Meanwhile the cit
Sees visions flit
Of contracts, stocks, and loans.
Thrice cent per cent   130
He grasps content;
He starts—awakes, and groans!

22

Lines

When the Devil was sick, the Devil a saint would be;
When the Devil was well—the Devil a saint was he.

Tradotto

Il diavolo ammalato
A Dio ben pregato
Gli accordar mercede—
Ma, ritorno in saluto,
Esser santo non voluto
Enega presto'l fede.

23

Epigram

From "Le Ramelet Moundi" by Godelin,
a poet who wrote in the dialect of
Thoulouse, early in the 17th century.

The gay, who would be counted wise,
Think all delight in pastime lies;
Nor heed they what the wise condemn;
Whilst they pass time—Time passes them.

Satirical Poems

24

Hame's the Best Place A'ter A'

Auld Nickieben ('twas in warm weather)
Assembled a' the de'ils thegither;
"An' weal enow," Auld Sooty cried,
"My louvin chiels, ye've stew'd an' fried—
You've had a bellyfu' o' brunstane,
An' hard your fate as ony whunstane.
I'll jist agen, as ance afore,
My luck in other realms explore,
An' aiblins, I moen find a biggin,
Mair cozie, chiels, for us to ligin."   10
The divels a' applaud his roavin—
Awa' he hied, then, at the gloamin.
He had na travell'd lang before
Three billies on a random splore
He met right luckie on his journey—
A parson, doctor and attorney;
They war indeed his ancien cronies,
A' mounted trig on Shetlan ponies.
The doctor in his knapsack carried
Physic for women—maids and married;   20
For men a bolus and a pill;
And a' he had could cure or kill.
But the puir lawyer naething hath,
Except the brass upon his face.
But that, they say, is a' in a'—
Without it law is naught ava'.
The priest, 'mangst ither things, had got
A buke he ca'd a polyglot,
An' tho' the buke o' truth he ca'd it,
It seem'd mair like [the] de'il had scraw'd it,   30
Sae fu' it was o' heathen Greek,
An' in sae mony tongues did speak.
The characters war a' sae crabbit,

Sae mixt the Hebrew wi' the Attic,
It wa'd ha'e puzzled Hugo Grotius,
Or, whilk is mair, the learn'd Duns Scotus,
Sae mony tongues there to unravel,
Strange an' as ancien' as auld Babel.
But tho' the saul was a' his hobby,
The priest was carefu' o' the body,   40
And in his pouch (a pious notion)
O' U. S. notes he'd a gude potion,
An' this he prov'd frae Paul the 'postle
At once was baith the law an' gospel.
But waes me, I maun tell my story—
The tale is lang an' a' before me.
The de'il was glad to meet the partie,
An' shook 'em by the neive right heartie.
"Heigh! sirs," he cried, "as sure as death,
To meet sic frens I'm naething laith.   50
Suppose we journey on thegither
An' mutually support each ither?"
Nae sooner said then 'twas agreed—
Each cavalier spurr'd on his steed.
Sair lang they travel slow an' fast
An' many a bonny prairie past.
At length (the de'il had heard its fame)
To happy Sangamon they came,
And ent'ring Springfield one cauld night,
At Jabez Capps' did a' alight.   60
Jabez—gude, hearty, honest fellow—
A groc'rie keeps, whar fowk get mellow;
Nane better in a lang day's ride,
And known to a' the country side.
Niest day they saunter thro' the town,
An' ilka thing they noted down.
The de'il beheld wi' joy the rabble
Drink, swear an' fight, an' gouge, an' scrabble.
"Weal done," he cried, "ye're jist yoursel',
An' like my ain sweet babes o' hell.   70
I fegs, I love ye quite as weal."

His comrades liked the country airie,
An' down they squatted in a prairie;
An' as they a' gat handsum fees,
They wived them soon wi' country shes.
The divel too was nation smart
An' quickly gain'd each female heart.
He in their bosoms aye was prying
An' gain'd them a' at ance by lying.
Na angel could like him succeed;   80
He was the very man indeed.
The tittering miss, the langing widow,
The divel, he was sure to win her.
He won them a' o' each degree,
An' a' was done by flatterie.
At last the de'il himself did wed—
But thorns are in the marriage bed.
She was a shrew that sairly vext him,
An' mair than hell itself perplext him.
An' tho' gude wives there are by dizens,   90
The divel found they a' war' cousins.
Then winter came in a' its rigor,
An' Sathan froze like any nigger.
Sae pinch'd wa' he by frost an' cauld,
He pin'd for his warm den o' auld;
So play'd his wife a Yankee trick,
An' aff he fled to hellward slick.
But then (to gie the de'il his due),
He left her pork an' meal enow.
She took anither, like the rest,   100
But a'ways swore that Nick wa' best.
Whan he came hame, gude Lord, what rout,
An' how the devils frick'd about.
Some twisted roun' like a tetotum,
Or scrad o' mutton when it's roastin,
An' a' belch'd out the fiery brunstane,
To show their dad that he wa' welcome.
They asked what foreign lands he saw,
An' if the fowk wa' fine and braw;

If he had seen the Yankee nation,   110
An' how he liked th' administration;
If fowks still crack'd o' Mrs. Eaton,
Wha put the presidential breeks on,
An' o' their auld friend General Jackson.
"Ah! weans," he cried, "now haud your jaw—
Hame is the best place after a'."

25

Cauld Comfort

Gie him gude drink
Until he wink.

Waes me, to think what men will do,
An' how they change frae auld to new.
The de'il ne'er starts a crazy notion
But, whoo, the fowk ar' a' in motion,
An' now they've taken arms an' swear,
Gude liquor they will taste nae mair—
An' wad ye think it, this cauld weather,
To live on water a'thegither?
Waes me, again, the very name
Curdles the blude thro' a' my frame.   10
Tak' ev'ry thing I love away,
But let me moisten well my clay—
Tak' pone, auld ned, tak' hommony,
(The de'il maun hae them a' for me;)
Tak' a' I hae—my weans, my wife;
Nay, ye may even tak' my life;
Afllict me wi' each human ill,
The lawyer's plea, the doctor's pill—
But let me hae my whiskey still!
Have ye nae mercie, nane at a',   20
An' will tak' each drap awa'?
Maun I ne'er taste o' co'niac
That gies the meagrims sic a smac,
An' when the cholic sairly pinches,
Maun I e'en die, ye Turks, by inches?
When a' my wean's in wild commotion,
Maun I ne'er taste o' rum a potion?
A feg for sic a heathen notion.
Suppose I meet a friend maist dear,

Wham I've not seen for many a year,   30
Must I sic friend at ance gae slau'ter,
An' gie him water, water, water?
Wad ye turn a' the warld to Quakers,
An' mak' men hypocrites an' Shakers?
An' know ye not, ye daft moon-rakers,
That those things which forbidden are
Each mother's son langs for the mair?
Now, tho' ye deem me a mere dunce,
Listen my frien's, wi' patience once,
Nor, at a jump, prohibit drinkin'.   40
Ye may as weel prohibit thinkin'.
Shou'd ye do baith, yet men wad think,
An' just as certain, they will drink.
If ye wad mak' an honest man,
(He may, or may not like a dram,)
Don't cram his mow wi' quiddilies,
Wi' auld wives' tales, an' dreams, an' lies—
Teach him to know himself, *"se ipse,"*
An' he will not be floor'd by whiskey.

26

To "The Prairie Bard"

Ye dinna ken, my rhymin' brither,
How glad I am to find anither
In this wild land o' boundless prairie,
(Waes me! at times I feel quite serie!)
Beside mysel', who spins a rhyme,
And dares the sacred mount to climb.
    I've seen your verses in the print,
And maun declare them of the mint—
Nae counterfeits, but current coin,
An' equal sense wi' sweetness join.   10
Now dinna think I mean to flatter;
Indeed, my fren', 'tis nae sic matter,
But I wad in my homely way
Unto your verse a tribute pay.
    I ken your town by distant fame,
An' faith, gude sir, it's got a name.
Fowk even say it dings out Springfield;
To that, indeed, I dare na yield.
It seems ye've built a famous college,
Brimfu' o' universal knowledge—   20
Besides an inn, so they relate,
O' inns the best in a' the state.
The last wi' heartfelt joy I hear,
For, truth to tell, I love gude cheer.
An' that, moreover, ye intend
To join our Springfield, end to end,
An' mak' a railroad to the river,
Like man an' wife, to jog thegither!
Wow! but it is a glorious motion,
An' shews ye hae nae common notion.   30
Gin ye will do it, I will make
A bran' new sang, jist for the sake.
They tell me too, ye're unco civil,

And do the gude—eschewing evil,
That in your town nae man gets drunk,
Nor can be found a single punk.
Heigh, sirs, that I could say as much
For Springfield, but I can't—in dutch!
I hear too, ye hae many anti's,
Besides a set o' dilettanti's,   40
Who in their lyceum do debate,
An' for your gude confabulate—
That to put down *all* inebriety
Ye've got an anti-tea society;
An' sair it puzzles me to think
What now your wives an' dochters drink.
Sweet, pretty dears—I fear they suffer,
And all my wean is in a flutter;
How do they eat their bread an' butter?
An' tell me what potation thin   50
Ye substitute for hyson-skin?
Should *we* do sic a thing, our wives
Wad fairly bang us a' our lives,
Sae much hae they o' fire and spirit,
An' sic a awfu' tongue inherit.
Here fowk eat bacon to satiety
In spite o' our auld ned society;
An' therefor I infer from this,
Your tariff against tea amiss.
There's ane thing I'd a'most forgot,   60
Tho' 'tis the best o' a' the lot.
It's tauld me that your better moiety
Hae form'd a pincushion society.
O ladies! I'm a single man,
An' humbly beg ye'll send me ane.
          But waes me, whither do I canter?
When I set out on this a'venture,
I tho't a verse or twa to make
Just out o' love an' rhymin' sake.
But sic a jade is my Pegassus,   70
She kicks and flings sae when she has us,

I can nae mair depend upon her
Than Punic faith or modern honor.
An' now I'll tell ye o' my whistle:
Tho' in my cap I wear the thistle,
And write in Scotch this plain epistle,
I still am o' the English breed,
An' liberty is aye my creed.
I mean plain liberty, the Quaker—
Not what some demagogues wad mak' her.   80
For her I left the island foggy,
Its gude roast beef and dumplins soggy,
To seek these wilds frae tyrants clear,
Another western pioneer.
     Now after this I needna say
Where tends the moral o' my lay—
That we maun all our spunk display
Our common country to embellish,
An' gie the true poetic finish.
There's few sae good a sod can boast,   90
How rich her fields, how fair her coast!
What store o' deer her woods maintain,
Turkies and every kind o' game!
Let us each hill and valley sing
And keep our fancy on the wing;
Describe the blooming prairie green,
As first in summer it is seen,
Deck'd out in flow'ers o' golden sheen;
When earth seems blended with the sky,
And the keen hawk is circling high,   100
Like death aroun' us hovrin' by.
Then mark what solemn thoughts inspire
To see our prairies a' on fire;
Or far off in the wilderness,
At midnight hear the wolf's distress.
A' these are subjects for the muse,
Nor need we other themes to choose.
Tho' weel she loves a foreign story,
Yet still at hame she rests her glory.

I dinna ken what streams ye claim,   110
Or if they yet have gat a name;
But there is ane, unless I err,
Your Morgan fowk ca' Mauvaise Terre.
Do thou in lofty rhyme exalt her,
An' cast your mantle on her water;
An' I will make our Sangamo
Outshine in verse the famous Po.

27

Huyler's Ghost

Who has not heard of Huyler? He was well known in Sangamo; and Springfield in particular was the scene of his exploits, where, *perhaps,* he drank more whiskey than any other man in it. But,

He is dead and gone—he is dead and gone.
At his head a grass-green turf, and at his heels a stone.
Shak.

Poor, harmless old man, and art thou indeed gone to thy rest—to thy narrow house—to thy long, long home? Thou didst drink, it is true; but, then, it was thine only failing, if, indeed, it could be called one in thee; for thou wast ever good natured in thy cups and, when drunk, wast most truly mellow. How many a gill have I drawn thee, and how didst thou once quaff the rich, old Monongahela! To thee it was sweeter than Rhenish; and when blushing with the rosy *Stoughton,* with what *gusto* wouldst thou swallow the capacious draught, ever courteously reminding me to add a *leetle* more and to be quicker nor shooting! But thou art gone! May the turf lie light on thy head, and may the refreshing dews of heaven (albeit thou lovedst not water in any shape) revive in the spring the green turf o'er thy grave!

The sun o'er Springfield long had set,
And night came on both cold and wet;
The wind in sudden gusts blew loud;
The sky was one dull sombre cloud;
Each rowdy now had gone to bed,
Or lain him by the fence instead;
The pretty misses home been squired,
And their fond lovers had retired
To store, to grocery or to shop,
Thinking the question how to pop;   10

When I, who by my waning fire,
Watch'd the embers slow expire,
Chewing the cud of sad reflection,
With many a pious interjection—
When thinking of the various freaks
And turns, which slippery fortune takes,
Just then, 'twixt sleeping and awaking,
Felt my shoulders gently shaking,
And looking up, who should I see
But Huyler, *in propria persona!*   20
Some fear I felt, but soon it fled,
While thus the sprite I questioned.
"By heaven and whiskey, tell me true,
Indeed, old boy, and is it you?"
"'Dis me, my werry self," it said,
"And now I speaks, although I'm dead.
Long in my doomb I'd quiet lain,
Nor fate allow'd me to complain;
But what is all dis stuff 'bout 'briety,
Waater and taamperance society?   30
The de'il himself, the black old tinker,
Dey say, has turn'd a water drinker;
And all his babes hab took to water,
Like ducks dat follow de old un after.
When I came into town dis night,
How dismal did appear the sight!
No jovial sounds fell on mine ear,
But all was flat and stale, like beer!
Not zo when I alive and vriskey
Guzzled each day mine quart o' whiskey,   40
And ere the rosy east was dawning,
Took my pitters in the morning."
(Bitters, the Dutchman meant—no matter,
I truly pen what he did utter.)
"Long had I wish'd again to see
Jabez Capps' old grocery,
And Rhadamanthus did implore
To let me take a glass once more."

I took the hint, and fill'd a gill,
With, "Here, old boy, now take your fill."   50
The sprite with ready zeal obey'd
And but a single gulp it made.
Gill after gill, the reeking tide,
Th' unwearied ghost I still supplied;
And, "Give me more—still more," it cried.
"Whiskey's a gure for every ill;
Libing or dead, I lub it still."
A gallon next, unto the brim,
I drew, and served it up to him.
Down sped the liquor sure and fast—   60
I thought he'd got enough, at last.
But no! the barrel, next he swore,
He'd drink before he'd pay the score.
So saying, out he whipt the bung,
And to his lips the barrel swung!—
When waking, for 'twas all a dream,
Methought I heard the owlet scream,
Then rubb'd my eyes and ope'd the door,
Just as McKenney's clock struck four.
I look'd toward the dusky wood,   70
Still in a hesitating mood,
And being yet with sleep opprest,
First trimm'd my fire, then sunk to rest.

28

To the Small Beer Poets

I'd rather be a kitten and cry mew,
Than one of those same metre ballad mongers.
Shakespeare

I'll tickle your cat-astrophes.
Myself

Of bards and cats, and such like stuff,
I think the town has had enough.
Old bachelors, a stubborn crew,
May love to hear their tabbies mew,
And doom'd to lead a single life,
Choose what is nearest to a wife.
'Tis but a cunning fetch of theirs
To gain th' affection of the fairs,
And by their love to tabbies show
How fierce the flame for *them* would glow.   10
But the chief diff'rence I can see
Is which's the most expensive she?
Now ladies, don't your bard condemn;
I'm just the same as other men,
And hold all cats in equal store,
Whether on two legs or on four.
That is to say, I love the sex,
Tho' cats will claw and women vex;
And if the first I do prefer,
I'll give the dears my reason there-   20
for————(oh, the rhyme!
How hard it is to make it chime!)
First, then, she's silent—(gift uncommon)
I never knew a silent woman;
And even men, though more profound,
In small talk and vile gab abound.

In the next place (for I love to be
Precise in my phraseology),
The cat's contented with her state,
And takes her seat beside the grate; 30
Her boarding too, it costs so little—
She only eats the broken vittle;
Besides, she's many a pleasing way,
And with her tail will oddly play;
And certes she does it mighty slick—
I wonder how she learnt the trick?
'Tis strange, but wheresoe'er I've been,
The same in every land I've seen.
Yes, we must love the household cat,
That keeps away the mouse and rat 40
That else would eat up all the meal,
And spoil whatever they can't steal.
Poor puss, her dress too ne'er abuses,
But her own homespun still she uses,
And keeps herself so neat and clean—
In maids and wives not always seen,
Unless upon some holiday;
Ah, then, indeed, 'tis who but they!
When ma'am, trick'd out in silks and laces,
Makes a thousand queer grimaces, 50
Her head she tosses high in air—
That makes the honest bumpkin stare—
And cocks her nose up so together,
Like pigs when they espy foul weather.
This sets your poetasters mad,
Who snort like calves that feel the gad;
And mounted on their own tame juckus,
Think all the while they stride Pegassus.
'Tis this inflicts the town with rhymes,
(When bad, the worst of all bad crimes,) 60
And thus they urge their splay-foot muse
(A jade the hell-man would refuse)
To cut such capers in the print
As if the very devil were in't.

And one, a drunkard's muse, thought fit
To palm on us another's wit.
Here hobbles out a vile iambic,
And there a limping dithyrambic,
With stophe and anti-strophe so put,
Like rams they do each other butt.   70
One pens a sonnet to his cat,
(By this we know what he'd be at;)
Why not another to a rat?
In this, at least, they'd be complete;
The subject would have equal feet,
As thus: the cat of feet has four;
The rat, I ween, can boast no more.
These added up in all make eight;
But who the de'il can count *your* feet?
   Oh, Springfield! fam'd for mud and beauty,   80
Why don't your poets do their duty,
And instead of verse to tabbies,
Write something *soft* to please the ladies?
One has indeed, in his small way,
Done something for the common clay.
Proceed, sweet bard, and sing the praise
Of woman, sweetest of all lays;
That purest porcelain of earth
(As Byron sings in canto fourth).
Alas, that I so old am grown,   90
Or else the theme were all my own;
For thus much of myself I'll say,
None better love that finer clay.
Sweet is the early breath of spring,
And streams in summer murmuring.
The rose is red, the lily fair,
And scent with balmy breath the air—
The rose and lily 's both combined
In those sweet dears called womankind.
No music like her voice I hear,   100
At once so bland, so soft, so clear.
And when a sidelong glance I spy,

Shot from a black or a blue eye
(For I'm not very nice in this—
Not grey, nor green, e'er come a miss),
I feel a something in me move,
Which if not love 's akin to love.
And when I lay me in my bed,
Soft visions float around my head.
Thames' lovely banks again I view,   110
And fondly deem the vision true.
Again I tread the well-known shore
That feels my bounding step once more;
Again unto my breast I strain
That dark-ey'd maid belov'd in vain;
But ah, the envious morning's nigh,
And I must wake to weep and sigh.
Alas, how bitter all the while
Is life, e'en when the most we smile!
Begun in mirth, 'tis clos'd in tears—   120
Thus ever end our mortal years.
A moment's space, a breath, a span,
Is all the gods allot to man.
O fool! to waste in idle rhyme
The hours that can no more be thine!
And this the vast result to be
Attained by greatest industry
(For like all arts, the art poetic,
If you'd obtain, you still must sweat it):
To make two lines together jingle,   130
When either would be better single—
Just like some marriages—enough!
Heu! heu! *jam satis—quantum suff.*

29

Bards and Reviewers

(Inscribed to the Critics)

I'll have some talk with this same learned Theban.
Shakespeare

Scruter, Scrutator, Scru—which is't
That you subscribe your classic fist?
I am not gifted sore with Latin,
But one or t'other 'tis, that's sartin.
Poeta nascitur, non fit—
Poets are born, not made—that's it.
This is the text from which you screw
Your hypercriticism through,
And to the modest bard dispense
Your critic bile—a mere pretence.   10
Horace should teach you better sense.
Besides, you mix up politics,
Just like "the devil on two sticks,"
And turning all things topsy-turvey,
You with the Bard attack th' attorney—
The de'il for this some day will burn ye.
Now answer me, I pray, good sir,
Why all this strife and mighty stir?
Why like a savage Mohawk come
To strike the tuneful brethren dumb?   20
And, with your club and scalping knife,
Threaten each gentle barding's life?
Why join with H., that renegado,
Who treats us like a Winnebago?
His was th' unkindest cut of all
Because it was poetical—
And what is more, 'twas rational;
But still a fratricidal blow,

Himself a brother barding too.
By this you may discern the British,   30
Who, like his nation, 's false and skittish,
And rather than a joke he'd smother,
Murder, in rhyme, his very brother!
'Tis true, he tickles us to death,
And tho' he kills, we needs must laugh!
But this is only more provoking,
And shews how fatal is his joking!
While you such heavy blows deal round,
The bruise is greater than the wound.
What have they done that you should be   40
To them so fierce an enemy?
If you don't like their simple lay
(Simple, indeed), another may.
You know the rule men go upon,
The maxim, *de gustibus non*—
What's one man's meat's another's poison.
Shakespeares, indeed, they may not be,
But still, they're poets in degree.
Milton's vast stores they don't possess,
And yet, they may not please the less;   50
Not do pretend within their scope
The ease and elegance of Pope.
Is there in verse no medium found,
But all must still be classic ground,
Sublime, most elegant, profound?
There are, besides the *dii majores*,
Or greater gods, the *dii minores*—
The lesser bards, as we may say,
Who deal but in the retail way.
We cannot all be Jabez Capps,   60
But still may sell good wine perhaps.
These are not poets quite, my master,
But may make up a poetaster.
Thus, it is said, nine tailors can,
When put together, make a man;
So these are pickayoon retailers,

Or small-beer poets, gentle readers,
Who with their rhymes amuse the town,
And like vile swipes, when dry, go down,
Or serve a more ignoble use—   70
What that may be, don't ask the muse.
Some please the farmer with their song,
In winter cold when nights are long—
I to this latter class belong.
Good, honest souls, I've heard 'em say
They làugh like mad at my poor lay,
And while the logs are burning clear,
Their boys and girls the tale will hear.
It pleases them to hear me sing
Because I touch on everything;   80
And I'm well pleas'd if but a smile
Reward me for my midnight toil;
And for their special use intend
To put the hard words at the end,
So that no diction'ry they'll need,
And, without spelling it, may read.
For I'm a poet popular
And love to write, but most of war;
And next to this, the ladies are
The lovely objects of my care.   90
When losing something of its fire,
For them I strike the willing lyre,
Or, lower yet a peg, confer
My service to the bachelor.
What though I boast not Byron's muse,
As varied as the rainbow's hues,
Nor dare compete with Tommy Moore,
I do my best—can you do more?
No, not in "jingletry," I snore!   100
        A bachelor, ah! wo the while!
Would fain the lonely hours beguile;
His tabby for a subject chooses,
And for her sake invokes the Muses—
Poor bard! you use him like a rat,

And worry him with his own cat.
Another pens a stave or two
To some fair maid—you stave him too!
A third (I hope it is not me),
Y' accuse of petty larceny;
And thus depreciate our ware—   110
Enough to make a parson swear!
Well, sir, to you this may be fun—
"Injuns!" I cry, "Give me my gun!"
Were I a bard like Mr. H.,
Who writes so elegant in Scotch,
I'd batter you all o'er with rhyme
For that same prosy piece of thine;
I'd scrutinize you, my Scrutator,
And rub you like a nutmeg grater.
My muse should be a porcupine   120
And set upon you with the Nine.
Lord! how I'd worry you, and flurry you,
Until you cried, "No more ado!"
'Tis bad enough to fight with hes;
What could you do 'gainst nine—all shes?
      Poets, you say, there are too many,
And grow like grass upon the prairie.
Well, what of that? Sure you should be
Glad of our soil's fertility,
Which with an equal hand diffuses   130
Such crops of statesmen, mud and muses,
Such as no other land can show
And only found in Sangamo—
Statesmen so fierce and patriotic
As shews the plant is no exotic,
But bred at home in our Far West
(As Yankees say down farther east,)
With mud so thick, so soft and dense,
It's only equall'd by their sense;
And muses such as can appear   140
In Springfield and no other where.
Raise our own poets! Is that wrong?

(No tariff needs the child of song!
And this, both Jackson-men and Clay,
I think, at least, will not gainsay.)
Why not raise poets, as well as pumpkins?
Is this your logic, Mister Tompkins?
And is it not much better far
Than to depend on foreign ware?
Let something of our Illinois   150
The poet's heart and verse employ;
Then, then you'll see him cock his eye,
Which will in a fine frenzy roll,
As Shakespeare says, from pole to pole:
"No! no! from heaven to earth, and then
From mother earth to heaven agen.
That is, my brother of the prairie,
From Jacksonville to Springfield fairly!
Ha! ha! this comes quite appropos
(Leave out the 's' and sound the 'o').   160
D'ye ken what's happ'd our Sangamo?
We've got a steamer, laddie, here!
When will you steam the Mauvais Terre?
I think, my fren', ye're unco blate,
For we've no heard frae ye o' late;
Or are too big and stalwart grown
My proffer'd love o' verse to own.
Gin that's your gate, my bonny bairn,
I hae a stomach like your ain;
I hantle verses just a wee   170
And am as proud o' them as ye.
You are The Prairie Bard, we know,
But I'm The Bard of Sangamo!"
This passing verse I thought was due,
And now I turn me to my Scru—
tater, it should be, but the rhyme
Must be lugg'd in some other time.
        Yes! e'en the boys would say 'tis fit;
We should encourage native wit,
Nor gang abroad to seek the stuff,   180

When at our doors we have enough.
Suppose it be not quite so fine
A thread as in those bards divine;
The coarser web for us will do.
It suits our back and pockets too;
And if but rude the humble rhyme,
It is not ruder than our clime.
Has not the bard already quoted
Declared our country should be noted?
And would you pluck his laurels down,   190
Which if not great, are all his own?
He that for Springfield has done more
Than ever poet did before,
Who always puff'd and prais'd her so
And the whole hog in verse would go;
And given our Sangamo a name
Immortal as the Po in fame.
In fifty thousand you think fit
T'assign to one the poet's wit—
You've reckon'd up the whole account   200
And shewn to what it does amount!
Indeed, you have a pleasant way
Your own hypothesis to lay,
And prove it true by algebra—
Thus Hudibras, that long of yore
High honors under Cromwell bore,
By merely looking at a flea
Could tell its weight by geometry.
So you, with equal skill, deduce
Springfield can't furnish out a muse;   210
Not ever can one poet bring
To touch with genuine fire the string,
And breathe a soul along the line,
Which if not quite, 's almost divine.
Well, be it so! Neither, my Scru,
Can we a critic boast in you!

30

On the Arrival of the First Steam Boat
(March 24, 1832)

If Jason, who the Golden Fleece
Sail'd for many years from Greece,
To such a height of fame did get
The Argonaut's remember'd yet,
Then what a debt of fame we owe
To him who on our Sangamo
First launch'd the steamer's daring prow;
Who first the unknown voyage sped,
And sailor like, went right ahead—
Nor cared, nor feared the dangers great   10
That on his devious course await—
But every obstacle withstood,
Frail ice, fall'n trees, and drifted wood,
Until he reach'd the distant strand
Where the great saw-mill points to land?
So Colon, by some Columbus nam'd,
This wondrous western world reclaim'd,
That erst lay hid from human ken,
Or only known to savage men;
Who o'er the waters vast and wide   20
The New World's happy shores descried,
And nam'd the land that first he saw
After his country, Hispaniola.
Be thine the praise, but not his lot,
For that was hard enough, God wot.
Henceforth shall Captain Pollock's name
Be blazon'd on the rolls of fame,
And latest generations know
What Bogue achieved for Sangamo.
Your Bard and prophet this presages: 30
Ye'll both go down to distant ages,

And like the Genoese of yore
Your fame will never die, I snore.
        Say, ye bold Springfield men, the sight—
Did it not give you vast delight?
And you fair dames, your comments on it;
It almost equall'd a new bonnet.
Could anything be so bewitching—
Lord, lord, to think on't sets me itching—
That is, in rhyme, my pretty dears,   40
As some one says some other wheres.
Both town and county went to see
What this strange animal could be,
But cautious first, and by degrees,
The Suckers peep'd behind the trees,
Till more familiar grown, they chase
And boldly stare her in the face.
One thought it might be Noah's ark—
"No, no," another did remark,
"Tis only Bogue's, his luck to try,   50
Nor need he here a dove let fly;
He only fears it should be dry!"
The news to Springfield quickly flew,
And all the folks went out to view
So strange a sight, to them so new;
Some thought the world was at an end,
And heav'n in mercy thus did send
To save the chosen people in
Who never yet committed sin,
Or only now and then got frisky   60
When broach'd an extra tub of whiskey.
Others there were who scouted this
And deem'd it all hypothesis—
Nor would their very eyes believe,
But cunningly themselves deceive.
"Twas all a flam," they said, "no doubt,
Or trick by th' Old One brought about."
They'd known such things before, they said,
And wisely look'd and shook the head.

These learned men from Jackson came,   70
That pious town of college fame,
Where thrifty Puritans resort,
Who love not steam of any sort—
Tis said they have their reasons for't—
And look on us with glance askew,
Because we are not thorough blue.
Ne'er mind, old Sangamo, a whit;
We'll give 'em all the go-by yet.
      Heigh, sirs, but I forgot to tell
What great rejoicing here befell.   80
Such stuffing—all the eggs in town
I do believe were then cram'd down—
And the next morn old ned quite high
Had ris'n in price, and none to buy.
There was a ball at night, I guess—
For th' ladies' sakes it couldn't be less—
And twenty bachelors, they say,
Were strung in Hymen's noose that day.
To such a height their courage went,
So tired were they of Love's long Lent!   90
Great guns were fired, and small ones too.
Believe me, Prairie Bard, tis true!
The ladies look'd no longer shy—
Dogs bark'd, cats mew'd, and boys did cry.
Our Bard, they say, e'en cock'd his eye,
And seemed a moment to beguile
His care-worn phiz into a smile;
And when he could no longer doubt it,
Made a bran' new song about it.
Jabez's gude liquors went off slick,   100
Some for the cash, but most on tick;
The small-beer poets made a show,
And their small whistles loud did blow,
But such a glance they got from Scru—
Away they scampered, *sauve qui peut!*
Like scattered deer, away they post;
'Twas then th' de'il take th' hindmost!

This I translate for honest men,
That all may know what 'tis I mean.
　　O thou! that o'er the prairie wild　　　　110
Presid'st, fond fancy's favorite child—
Who whilom I did pen a stave to
By way of friendly "How d'ye do!"
What think ye, laddie, isn't it grand
To see a steamer touch our strand?
Didn't I tell ye lang ago
How high would reach our Sangamo,
And is it not like gospel true
What then I did propose to you?
I've kept my word, like a true Briton.　　　　120
See the western wilds I've writ on
In answer to a pleasant ditty
By a fair lady of the city
Who thinks our western wilds are sad.
You think not so, my bonnie lad—
Nor wad she either, did she know
How great our joy in Sangamo.
She gain'd a prize, too, for her freaks,
And I, galore, a pair o' breeks,
Which they presented to the chiel　　　　130
Because they think he sings sae weel.
But you, ye dinna say a word—
Nor of your steamer have we heard!
Do take your pen and let us hear
How gangs she up the Mauvaise Terre—
Then we'll compare notes and see
If both our Talismen agree.

31

The Remonstrance

When I said I would die a bachelor,
I did not think I should live till I were married.
Shakespeare

There are, who think I should essay
Something of love's propitious sway:
    "And why not, for the fair awhile,
    Resign," they cry, "this biting style?
    These bitter strains will never do,
    And what is worse, they are so true.
    If you broach'd nothing else but lies,
    It never would the town surprise,
    But when you dare to speak the truth,
    It is too much for them in sooth.   10
    Hath Venus then, her charms, no power
    To lure thee to her myrtle bower?
    Did Cupid never cause thee smart,
    Nor wound that hard, obdurate heart?
    Can't the soft cares of love alarm
    Thy sullen breast, nor beauty charm,
    That still to satire you must turn,
    And laugh at love, when you should burn?
    Harder than brass that breast must be,
    Which owns no kind, controlling she;   20
    And scant the praise you'll e'er obtain,
    Unless to love you turn the strain.
    By love hath Ovid got a name,
    Byron, and Tommy Moore the same.
    Fame is a female goddess known;
    No wonder, then, she likes her own.
    Behold the maids our Springfield boasts:
    Are they not all the reigning toasts?
    Like stars that form the Milky Way,

Their brightness emulates the day.   30
Behold them in the mazy dance,
How gracefully they do advance!
Just like some creatures of the air,
So light, so bright, so tight, so fair;
Or Houries, that in paradise
The holy Musselmen entice;
Or sylphs, that float in visions bright
Before the poet's raptur'd sight!
No soft Italian maids can vie
With those that grace our Illinois;   40
Nor France, tho' supple jointed, prove
A match for our sweet girls in love!
Can'st thou such lovely forms behold,
And yet remain like stoic cold?
Surely, if such fair maids can't charm,
Love, nor the devil himself, can warm."
I answer them, as well I may,
That love with me has had his day;
That my poor heart is like the pumice
The fire turns out o' Mount Vesuvius—   50
So scorch'd, and such a cinder made,
It's all too cool for love's warm trade.
Besides, now that the old heat's out,
I think more of the where-about—
So, when a charming fair I see,
Think how expensive she must be;
And when deck'd out in all her colors,
"Good Lord," I cry, "what waste of dollars!"
I like, indeed, a sparkling eye,
But just as well a beef steak pie!   60
And if miss sports a handsome toe,
I know it to the ball will go!
What, though in dancing she's complete,
Will that buy bread and butcher's meat?
And, tho' a sylph she may appear,
These sylphs expensive silks will wear;
And to their loss, some poets know,

When wedded, they have wedded woe!
In evil hours their time did barter,
And for an angel got a Tartar—   70
Houries, indeed, that's something new;
Perhaps it's Turkish for a shrew!
Yet, the plain truth to tell, a wife
Is a great blessing in this life—
I mean when we can get a good 'un,
One that knows how to make a pudden;
Whom vanity nor spleen o'er reaches,
And, in a pinch, can mend your breeches;
Who takes a world of pains to please,
Nor thinks it is her right to tease.   80
It is the natural state of man
To tack himself unto a 'oman;
And, therefore, nature owes a spite
To such as shun the marriage rite.
Witness these frisky bachelors
Whom *ennui,* the fiend, devours,
How thin they be, how dry and spare,
As if oppressed with every care;
How listless they appear all day,
And then, at night, how mopish they.   90
They from themselves would seem to fly,
Seeking the other moiety—
For man, they say, is woman too,
Or, rather, she is man also,
The half of him, join'd by a ring,
A softer male, or some such thing;
Which, tho' they separated be,
Are still of one affinity;
And these two halves together make
But one, when better for worse they take.   100
The other moiety, it's true,
But flies that this may more pursue,
Which of itself would seem to prove
That men should woo, and women love.
    This seems to be the real intent

Of Nature, and is what she meant,
For that which is enjoyed by one
Is the same as if enjoy'd by none.
Single, your joys are single too—
Married, each other they renew.   110
How pleasant! to myself I've said,
When to some cot, that love hath made,
At eve I've seen the husband come,
By his kind partner welcom'd home—
Welcom'd with looks, and loving smiles,
That well repay his daily toils.
A blazing fire is on the hearth;
Around it, cheerfulness and mirth;
His children in wild transports play,
And he's as much a child as they.   120
Meanwhile, the supper she prepares,
And plies full well her household cares;
The decent table cloth is laid,
And with her choicest viands spread;
Yet she herself will scarcely sit,
But helps him to the nicest bit.
Happy, thrice happy, is the man
Whom fate hath given such a 'oman!
Fortune may frown; within her breast,
There, there he has a friend at least—   130
Nor death itself can sever quite
The cords that such fond hearts unite.
        But see, the bachelor, how grim!
No wife prepares the hearth for him;
No prattling children round him play
To win him from his cares away;
No smoking dishes grace his board;
No nice tit bit for him is stored;
Or if a crust hath chanc'd to stray,
Tabby hath clear'd it all away.   140
The very cat hath left his door,
And better loves the streets to scour
Than to abide in such a place,

And never see a female face.
No crickets sing around his walls,
But Malkin to Grimalkin squalls.
By his low fire he sits all sad
(For what can make his spirit glad?)
And listens to the midnight breeze
That dies away by slow degrees;   150
Or hears the am'rous cats at play—
Himself not half so blithe as they;
Then stalks around his lonely room,
Wrapt in sad thought, and night, and gloom,
And, as the fitful breezes sigh,
The ghosts of other days pass by.
Slowly they rise before his sight,
And double horrors give the night—
Sweet girls, whom once he knew full well,
And told them many a lying tale,   160
Which they believ'd in silly sooth—
So much doth flatt'ry look like truth;
In all their beauty they appear,
Only a little th' worse for wear.
These haunt him now in wicked dreams,
And mingle with the night their screams;
So fancy, to his guilty mind,
Shapes the low moanings of th' wind,
Or those shrill notes that Tabby swears,
And growls into her lover's ears   170
When in the dark they meet together,
And spit their loves at one another.
And one there is, among the rest,
Who beats with rage her jealous breast.
No tender love-lorn maid is she,
But rather, one whom love would flee—
A bold virago, fierce and stout,
Who'd break your head, or teeth knock out,
And little of her sex did shew,
Except that she could snivel too.   180
This vixen seems to hold him close,

And round him deal her handy blows;
When stretching out his foot in ire,
He pokes it in the reeking fire!
Roaring with pain, he draws it out,
And in wild antics frisks about.
At last unto his bed he creeps,
But 'tis not often there he sleeps,
Or if, a while, he close his eyes,
Fancy the waking sense supplies.   190
In love's own merry month of May,
Through flow'ry meads he seems to stray.
Soft is the genial air around,
And soft the whisp-ring woods resound;
Roses and lillies deck the scene,
Prank'd out in nature's lively green;
While heav'n, and earth, and love conspire
To set his yielding heart on fire.
In this soft paradise he strays,
As he was wont in happier days,   200
And at his side, no longer shy,
The blue-ey'd maid is standing by,
The same in look, and voice and mien,
As she appeared at sweet sixteen,
When love is loveliest, I ween;
But whilst he hugs this heav'n of charms,
Wakes with the bed post in his arms!
Or varying, still, the dreams of night,
He hears her to another plight
The vows that should be his by right.   210
Then jealous rage his heart assails,
And fiercely at the sex he rails—
Vows he will live a single man,
Nor ever yoke himself to woman;
He hates the sex, he falsely swears,
Yet all the while, he loves the dears!
And rather than live single, he
Would hang, or drown, or poison'd be.
        Here had I ended, but the Muse

Whisper'd a trick that's now in use—   220
Lord, Lord, what will not man essay
When with the gals he 'gins to play?
'Tis said they have a magic hoop,
In which the ladies they would coop,
Who, like wild fillies, fearing naught,
By the wily bachelors are caught,
And once within the wooden ring,
Are kiss'd—howe'er they kick and fling!
A fine invention this, no doubt,
To bring the grand affair about!   230
Ah! little do they think the while
How on themselves may turn the guile.
Like all things smacking of the yoke,
The ladies much admire the joke,
And think how in their turn they'll fix
A tougher round their husbands' necks.
Wisely the ancient saying went:
"Single or married, you'll repent."

32

Lament for the Small Beer Poets

O whither fled, sweet bards, that erst
Were with such fits of rhyming curst—
Ah, whither fled? Shall we no more
Sing your love-lorn ditties o'er,
Nor listen to your sprightly strains,
The pride of all our Sucker plains—
Sweet strains that charm'd the whippoorwill,
And made the catbird own your skill;
Nay, rivall'd e'en the kitty did
So easy into verse they slid?   10

      Say, hath Scrutator screw'd you down
That you no more amuse the town;
Veto'd the issue of your brains
(The product of such mental pains,)
That still would wriggle into life
Like tadpoles when the Spring is rife?
Or did you quit yourselves the verse,
At once so vari'd, strong and terse,
And like a child, with rattle tired,
Threw by what once [you] had admired?   20

      Tell me, ye journeymen of song,
To whom the Muses' task belong,
Where are those tropes and similes
That stood as thick as leaves on trees,
And with such beauty could dispense
Alike with wit and common sense?
For what had you to do with those,
The common attributes of prose?
O why are you so silent all?
No sonnet, song or madrigal   30

The *Journal* ever boasts from ye,
And I am left alone, perdie!

     Do subjects lack to point your quill?
O, bards awake! We've tabbies still!
These once awoke the tender strain
And may inspire your harps again;
Or if that subject's rather flat,
You can another choose. The rat
May all your inspiration share.
We have them yet, and some to spare.   40
These haunt the bar, the store, the shop,
Nor even at the pulpit stop—
Rats of all sizes and degrees,
Besides the rogues that nibble cheese.
But you, perhaps, a wife have got.
If so, indeed, God help your lot!
The Muse and marriage ill agree;
Squalls suit not well with poetry.
Nor can your wife, however kind,
At times restore a troubled mind.   50
A critic sour she'll be to you—
Perhaps another female Scru.
And those sweet pledges of your love—
By some call'd brats—may noisy prove;
For while you beat your empty brain,
And find all knocking there in vain,
Dick kindly gives a hint instead
And sends a stone right at your head,
Whilst Moll, on equal mischief bent,
In your best coat a hole hath rent,   60
Or poked a sonnet in the fire,
Where now the last sad lines expire.
But these are trivial cares, you'll say.
Imagine, then, a washing day,
When all the hell of soap and suds
Assail you from infernal tubs!
But if, inspired by all the nine,

You sit at ease, nor whince, nor whine,
Alas, poor man, thou still must dine!
No Muses then can give relief;   70
More need hast thou of solid beef.
And tho' the pure Castalian stream
May figure in a poet's dream,
He'd give the whole, and more, I fear,
For a good draught of Pittsburgh beer.

Poems on Nature

33

The Western Wilds

*Suggested by some verses on the same
subject by Mrs. Sigourney.*

Who says our western wilds are sad?
    Who sings so faint a lay?
What scene can make that spirit glad
    Which here cannot be gay?

Behold our prairies spreading wide;
    In spring how green they be;
The gallant steeds that o'er them ride,
    Away, exulting free!

And he who strides the gallant steed
    A deeper joy must know,   10
With heaven's own blue above his head,
    And earth's bright flow'rs below!

How fresh, careering o'er the wild,
    Our western breezes play!
The heavy heart of care's beguil'd,
    And leaping, hails the day!

Behold the mighty streams that lave
    The wild Missouri strand,
Or our more lovely Illinois—
    The beautiful, the grand!   20

The deer is seen at peep of morn,
    The wolf at close of day;
And merry sounds the hunter's horn
    When he brings home his prey.

And see! our rugged prairie men;
        O, who more free than they?
They're tall, they're stout—they ne'er give out;
        Who dares them to the fray?

Fair stranger! keep thine own fire-side;
        Such scenes are not for thee.   30
They're stern, indeed, who here abide,
        But, then, how bold and free!

I blame you not because you love
        The gentler scenes of home
And cannot here the comforts prove
        Which they must leave who roam.

I, too, have known the city's pride,
        And in a fairer land—
Give me the prairie, green and wide,
        Fresh from th' Almighty's hand.   40

No slaves beneath the tyrant's yoke
        Here wear their lives away,
Nor vengeance from the gods invoke
        And, sighing, curse the day;

But free as the wild winds that sweep
        Along our boundless plains
Are we, and still the boon will keep,
        While earth—while heav'n remains.

34

Lines on the Approach of Winter

In the spring the violet blows—
Summer claims the blushing rose;
But, when cool September's near,
When the leaf looks sad and sere,
Then farewell the violet blue—
Farewell the rose and lily too!
Untimely cropt, they fade away,
To bloom again another May!
So the fair maid, whose early doom
Consigns her to the silent tomb,   10
But leaves this narrow world's confine
To bloom again in bliss divine.
Now the wild prairie to the view
Appears in autumn's sober hue—
And, past her summer's flow'ry pride,
Looks like some lone and widow'd bride—
'Till at last, advancing cold,
Another season we behold,
And instead of lively green
The winding sheet of winter's seen.   20
Now piercing winds, and driving hail,
The weary, wandering wretch assail—
Who hails with joy the friendly light
That guides him in his course aright.
Yet tho' the winds are piping loud,
And Nature wears her fun'ral shroud,
This is the time when honest cheer
Greets with smiles th' op'ning year.
The logs are piled upon the hearth,
And all is joy and thoughtless mirth;   30
The sparkling ale with glee goes round,
Till in large draughts each care is drown'd;
The bashful maid the goblet sips—

Not half so tempting as her lips—
And silent, speaks in glances shy
To the glad youth assiduous by.
The farmer tells th' oft-told tale;
His neighbors praise the cakes and ale;
The childen with the kittens play,
As wild, as frolicsome as they;   40
And garrulous, the old relate
The marvels of their younger state;
While the good housewife on the board
Displays her nuts for winter stored.
Without, the storm is raging high,
And man and beast to covert fly—
All but the wolf with hunger keen,
Who howls his lonely watch between—
But little heed they of the din
While all is snug and warm within.   50
Tho' still, at times, the tear will rise
For those who brave the angry skies;
And, pointing to the vacant seat,
Confess their joy as incomplete.
Sweet power, that for another's woe
Prompts the feeling tear to flow,
May I ne'er shut my heart to thee,
For what is life but sympathy?

35

Winter Nights

These sullen hours—how heavily they pass
When the black clouds, big with autumnal floods,
Upon the earth pour all their store of rain;
And Illinois, all reeking with soft mud,
Makes it full difficult to plough your way;
For wheresoe'er you turn the slippery road,
You stand engulphed, confounded in the mire—
A spectacle most pitiful to see.

O give me winter! Winter clear and cold!
When the blue sky shines in the heavens serene,   10
And the hoar frost lies light upon the ground,
Then are the nerves well strung, the spirite light,
The step elastic—and the bracing air
Puts life into the heart, and to the limb,
As o'er the prairie swift, on horse or foot,
You joyous go, nor heed the blustering North.
Let the winds rave—I love the rushing blast
That beats against my door, but comes not in.
Meanwhile secure, I sit before the fire,
With hickory or solid oak well piled,   20
And in the embers view phantastic shapes
Of regions wild and wondrous, many a scene;
Or haply, with a book, beguile the hours—
A book of knights and arms, and tourneys rare,
Such as dan Spenser sings or modern Scott.
But tired, at last, with fancy's unreal feast,
From its warm berth I reach the lusty haunch
That graces well my ample chimney's side—
A store reserv'd for winter's hungry nights—
And cutting off a slice or two, not thin,   30
Laid on the glowing coals they soon are done.
These I wash down with Mon'gahela good,
Then trim my lamp, and tumble into bed.

36

Winter

Now comes the winter cold; the dying year
Gives notice of its fall; the leaves, all sere,
Strew the lone pathway of the dim dun wood
Where the lithe squirrel now lays up its food.
Cold chilling winds prevail; the drizzling rain
Falls sad, and drenches all the dusty plain.
Ill fares the traveller now who, far from home,
Or inn, the weary road is forced to roam—
While night surrounds him, and he's lost his way,
Or (what is worse) in pouch there's nought to pay.   10
How pleasant looks the parlor's blazing grate,
Where the blithe guests the merry tale relate;
But he, poor wight, slinks sad away from view,
Watching the frowning landlord's looks askew,
As tired he stands with stick and chattels few.
O, ye good Christians, who in churches pray,
Don't turn the weary traveller away;
But think upon your Master who, like him,
Journeyed this wicked world of woe and sin—
And if the temperance pledge ye have not taken,   20
Give him a dram, a bed, and slice of bacon.

37

Wolves

In this dread season, when the leafless trees
Shew winter's rage, and the keen, cutting wind
Blows fierce and fell across the prairie wild,
How pleasant to repose secure at home,
And listen to the savage din abroad.
But ah! how fares it with the traveler now,
Who late, and wandering in a region strange,
Sees nought but level snow before him lies,
As oft he pauses—dubious of the road—
While night's dim curtains darkly close around—   10
Then desperate plunges through the snowy waste,
No path to guide him, and no fire to warm;
Till down he sinks at last, and black despair
Brings hideous shapes and fancies to his eyes.
Meanwhile, faintly at first, and mingled with the blast,
The long, loud howl of wolves upon his track
Is now distinctly heard.———
Ah me! what horror then his soul alarms,
As nearer, and more near, he sees them come,
Their dusky forms contrasting with the snow,   20
While open-mouth'd, and ready to devour,
Their green eyes fasten on their destin'd prey.
No help is nigh—to heaven he calls in vain—
While the pale moon, as if to mock his woe,
Shines calm and cold upon the pallid scene.

38

When Will the Spring Return?

Too much of sleet, of cold and rain,
Too much of winter's drear domain,
A hideous waste lies all the plain.
         When will the spring return?

The merry birds are heard no more,
The woods are robb'd of all their store,
The fields with snow are covered o'er.
         When will the spring return?

Mournful among the leafless trees
Is heard the sighing of the breeze,   10
And every sight and sound displease.
         When will the spring return?

When will the fields again be green,
And Nature's lovely face be seen,
Soft sunny days and nights serene.
         When will the spring return?

When will the birds again rejoice,
The nightengale lift up her voice,
The flowers expand, with all things choice.
         When will the spring return?   20

Released from out this prison cold,
Ah, when shall I the sun behold,
That tops the eastern hills with gold?
         When will the spring return?

Sad is the clime where winter reigns,
And cold as is their icy plains
The hearts that dwell in his domains.
      When will the spring return?

Ah me, my country! when once more
These wandering feet shall press thy shore,   30
Then, then indeed, and not before,
      Then will the spring return!

39

Vernal Musings

i grati zeffiri di primavera.
Metast.

Now that the gentle Spring again
Renews in all her pride the plain—
When the soft buds are bursting free
From bush and brake and forest tree,
And the blue violet is seen,
Peeping beside the vernal green;
When birds are vocal in the wood,
And cheer each lonely solitude;
Then from the town I take my way,
And through the pleasant prairie stray,   10
Nor shun the turbid steams that creep
Their noiseless course round hillocks steep,
And mark the frog leap nimbly by
Whene'er my step approaches nigh.
Or, roaming further in the shade,
I meet, at times, a lonely glade,
Where the young grass a fresher green
Throws around the sylvan scene;
Or rest upon a fallen tree
That makes a rustic seat for me;   20
Then musing on the days gone by,
As fancy prompts the smile or sigh,
So to my wandering muse impart
The comic, or the tragic part;
Or, lost in a poetic dream,
I watch the windings of the stream,
And, moralizing in my way,
Compare the past and present day.

Here rov'd, and not far years agone,
The prairie's wild and native son,   30
Who by the chase procured his food—
The untaught savage of the wood.
Here, on this very spot, I cry,
He made the bear or panther die;
And here, perhaps, his wigwam rude
Arose upon the solitude.
But now, within the sylvan scene,
The white man's paler face is seen,
And where the buffalo and bear
Late roam'd, arises Springfield fair,   40
And all the arts of civil life
Within the little town are rife,
And in its narrow precincts found
The products of the world around.
From farthest Ind the silk appears,
That here the charming Sucker wears;
While England's toiling race supply
The knife that desolates the sty;
Here, many thousand miles, is brought
What constitutes our morning draught,   50
And, further still, from old Cathay,
The herb that makes our evening tea—
Besides whatever else we owe
To our own matchless Sangamo;
And this the vast result at last:
To eat old ned and corn—or fast!
Or, if a tough beef steak we choose,
It choaks the poet and his muse.
What muse but mine could keep her wing,
Or on such beggar's fare could sing?   60
As for old ned, a kind of food
That never does a poet good,
To live on that, it makes me mad,
Or, like a small-beer poet, sad;
And I could do a desperate thing—
Be wived, or dangle from a string!

Give me, ye gods, of beef enough,
And, oh, don't let it be so tough.
My muse is no aerial sprite,
But solid pudding 's her delight.   70
Hers are no wishy-washy strains
That's fed on sentimental pains;
Nor is she of that sober crew
For whom the water pure will do;
But give her wine her soul to cheer,
Or even humble Pittsburgh beer,
And add to that a pound or so
Of good beef steak—she'll make it go.
With such a meal, she'd raise a note
That could resound to lands remote,   80
And all the 'varsal world should know
How lives the Bard in Sangamo.

Sweet name! like music heard at night;
The very sound yields me delight;
So strong, so soft, so every thing—
'Twas made on purpose I should sing!
Here spreads the prairie, wild and free,
A charming sight it is to see,
When Spring her cloak of living green
Lays out beneath the sunny sheen,   90
And the tall flowers deck the ground,
Like lovely Suckers smiling round.
Come from the East, come from the West,
All you that seek a heaven of rest.
Ye weary wights, no further go,
But pitch your tents in Sangamo.

40

To the Frogs

Again sweet warblers of the spring,
Your jovial throats in concert ring,
And from the yielding mud around,
All vocal made, your songs resound,
A sure presage that winter hoar
Deforms the opening year no more.
Now bursting buds the trees adorn
That lately look'd like men forlorn;
The streams, releas'd from icy chains,
Run murmuring along the plains;   10
Soft balmy breezes in the wood
To life awake the callow brood;
And, changing all the wint'ry scene,
The prairie re-assumes her green.
    Now, with the Muses by my side,
I love to rove at morning tide,
Or, in the still and quiet eve,
The close and crowded town to leave,
And stroll, all careless, lone and free,
Where none are found to stroll but me,   20
In that sweet shade which evening lends,
Ere yet with night complete it blends,
While all is mute and still beside,
Save the low ripple of the tide
Of some lone, winding creek that strays,
And in the last faint sunshine plays.
But, when awhile you cease the strain,
Methinks I hear a voice complain—
A gentle voice, which like the sigh
The zephyrs breathe when roses die,   30
Or those sweet sounds we often hear
In depth of woods or waters clear—
Soft, gentle sounds, we scarce may tell
Or sad or gay, yet please they well.
Anon, strange shapes methinks I see,

That bear Titania company!
An elfin troop, all fair and bright
As ever tripp'd in the pale moonlight
By Thames or Avon's fairy bowers,
Or old Tintaggel's ruin'd towers;   40
But all an Indian aspect wear,
And in the Indian garb appear—
These, the bright maids that long ago
Liv'd, breath'd and mov'd in Sangamo!
Black are their raven locks as night,
Their sun-burnt cheeks all red bedight,
With buskin'd feet that deftly move
In that grave dance the Indians love.
Well pleas'd they look and softly smile,
The small bells jingling all the while;   50
Flash their dark eyes the living fire
Of love, and youth, and fond desire,
As oft, upon the favor'd one
They glance, and meant for him alone;
While many a dusky form is there
Of mighty chiefs, that bravest were;
Couch'd on the grass, their arms not far,
And ready for the instant war.
At intervals the moon between
Casts a pale light upon the scene.   60
        Again you croak—then all is gone!
And I am musing here alone
On that wild race, whose destiny
Awakes the heart's best sympathy;
And while I wend my homeward way,
I pensive ask, "Now, where are they?"
Far has the pale-fac'd stranger driven
The Indian from his native heaven;
No more in Sangamo we see
That noble race—the Illinee!   70
And if a few on earth remain,
They see not Illinois again!
Far up the wild Missouri's banks they roam,
Or Mississippi, find a foreign home.

41

The Indian

I sat beneath a pawpaw tree
    Beside Ohio's stream,
Reflecting how my life had been
    Nothing but a dream!

And as I sat and gaz'd around
    With sober thought and eye,
An Indian came and crouch'd him down,
    Then heav'd a bitter sigh.

"See'st thou this stream, these fields, these trees
    That bend a grateful shade?   10
They once were ours," the Indian said,
    "And every pleasant glade.

The white man came—he took them all;
    He drove our race away,
And now we wander sad, forlorn,
    Where sinks the western ray.

E'en thence they chase us, and our doom
    It needs no seer to see:
The white man wants more elbow room;
    We perish in the sea!"   20

42

Sonnet to the Frogs

Tired with yawning over the fire in my little back parlor last Sunday—reading the productions of the small-beer poets and comparing one cat-muse with another—I wandered forth into the woods that so agreeably skirt our thriving little town, and while contrasting in my mind the pleasant aspect they presented last summer with their present desolate appearance, I was glad to hear again the cheerful notes of the frogs—those mellifluous harbingers of spring and warm weather. I had, indeed, been told that their sweet voices were heard as much as a week before, but the person who related this extraordinary event being a poet, I looked upon his assertion as a mere flight of fancy—the natural effect of an overheated imagination; but now I could not be mistaken, as I heard them with my own proper ears, which are large and capacious, like those of a certain animal whose name I don't choose to mention, and at the same time quick as those of Huindal, the porter of Valhalla, who could hear the grass grow in the meadow, and the wool on the back of sheep. Here, then, after taking a few turns up and down my accustomed walks of last autumn, and noting the sad effects which the late winter had caused among the ranks of my old companions, the trees, I at last seated myself on a stump, and gathering under me the skirts of my green great coat, to make the set more easy, I presently fell into an agreeable reverie—when among other things, these pretty verses of Leander came into my mind: "The world *(id est,* Springfield) is full of poetry." If this be so, said I, at the same time unconsciously giving vent to one of those monologues in which I so often indulge, even in the very precincts of that sanctuary of drink and dry goods yclept Capps' Grocery—surrounded as I am all the day long by the brawling votaries of Bacchus, or whiskey rather, for that is the proper name of the Sucker-god of guzzle—if this be so, says I, why, then, may not these innocent warblers, who sing so sweetly in their own native mud, be poets, or at least poetasters? And, surely, the poetry of the frogs, says I again, must be at least as agreeable as that of the cats! And if there be poets in the ditches, then why not critics too! Yes, sartinly, it's as clear as mud; and I was the more confirmed in this opinion as I could, at times, distinguish a pause in the wood notes wild of these independent choristers, which was always preceded by a gruff, surly kind of croaking, that sounded in my ears like the language of scorn and contempt, and which interrupted, for a while, the sweet flow of song—but only for a while, as it was invariably followed by a strain of fresh sweetness and vigour, as if in despite of the harsh reproof of the critic; for this lugubrious note could only proceed from some Scrutator of the ditch. Whereupon, musing on this singular coincidence, and throwing my legs across like a Knight Templar, a certain sign with me of the divine afflatus (for so I think Mr. Scru calls it, but which in plain English is only a sort of swelling or puffing up of wind), I seized incontinently my harp—yes, gentle reader, my harp—a real bona fide harp, and no vain coinage of the brain. It was a jew's harp, by the bye, and won by me from a New England pedlar in a fair contest of *hyme* singing; when like good King David of old—as represented in an ancient cut to my Dutch version of the psalms, by that ingenious artist, Nicholas Van Schlotterbaum, who adorns the royal minstrel with an ample pair of yellow breeches, garnished at the knees with a bunch of red ribbons, enormous buckles in his shoon, and a bob wig—I composed and sung, at the same time accompanying it with my lyre or harp, the following:

Ye jovial croakers, who salute the spring
In that soft Dutch by mortals call'd "the low,"
I hear, indeed, your pleasant warble-ing,
But what 'tis all about would like to know!
Perhaps, in your harmonious songs so sweet,
Ye tell of vernal blooms and meadows green,
And how, since fled the wintry snow and sleet,
Ye hail with tuneful throats the alter'd scene.
Beware, my friends, nor raise too high the song,
For we have critics in the neighbor town—   10
Sad fellows these, as ye may know ere long,
Who run each gentle warbling croaker down;
And should you meet with him they call the Scru,
Fly, fly, begone! or he may swallow you.

43

Sonnet

Still lingers winter; and the blust'ring wind,
As loth to part, fierce o'er the prairie blows.
Cold from the North, that prison-house of snows,
He comes, and leaves the timid spring behind.
Yet, for a space, the genial sun will shine,
But, like a treach'rous friend, when fortune lowers,
So faint his beams that you almost repine,
Knowing full well he brings but wintry showers.
Cold in the joyous woods is now the air,
Where the dead leaves in heaps promiscuous lie;   10
Aloft the branches wave, all lone and bare,
And through the leafless boughs the night-winds sigh.
Sad is the scene throughout, and ill at ease
The traveler who wends through ways like these.

44

The Approach of Spring

i grati zeffiri di primavera.

Now from the south the genial breezes blow,
Dissolving winter's horrid front of snow;
The fields again emerge, but brown and sere,
Disrobed of all their beauty they appear.
Waked into life the birds begin to sing,
Or try, at least, a kind of twittering;
The streams are loose, while here and there is seen
Something that looks as if it might be green.
The mud is everywhere, and in the sty
The sow and all the little ones are spry.   10
Now in the town the dapper clerk appears,
Early to rise, with quill behind his ear—
The loafers all are out the sun to meet,
And politicians buzz in every street.
Sweet faces now are seen along the way;
The beaus are smart, and hens begin to lay.

45

Sonnet

i grati zeffiri di primavera.
Metast.

The gentle Spring, soft breathing, dropping flowers
From out her ample lap, a bounteous store,
Invites my steps abroad to her green bowers,
Studious again to scan her beauties o'er.
Softly the zephyrs round my temples play,
As o'er the green, where peeps the violet blue,
At early morn I take my devious way,
And mark each lovely object in the view.
The woods again put forth their lovely green,
While their sweet tenants hail the jocund morn;   10
Around, above, below, fresh life is seen;
The flowers give out a smell, the plum tree and the thorn;
And every thing that breathes the vital air
Confess the genial reign, and murmur forth a prayer.

46

Sonnet

The sullen hours on leaden pinions fly,
And the warm air betokens coming rain;
Low heavy clouds hang o'er the northern sky,
And grunting hogs scud homeward might and main.
The sheep, loud bleating, hasten to the fold;
The cows return, and now are Dolly's care;
The busy housewife's often heard to scold
While hungry bairns cry for their evening fare.
Now night descends; the dark'ning shadows fall
On hill, on tree, on cot, on prairie wide;   10
The dog barks at the traveller, and the squall
Of bairns is hushed—asleep by daddy's side.
Fond love-sick swains dream of the fair one's charms,
And Tabby flies to her Grimalkin's arms.

47

Sonnet

Fierce overhead the fervid dog-star reigns,
And level downward rays the fields consume;
Nature, aghast, falls fainting on the plains,
And the fair flowers lose all their sweet perfume.
The weary reaper hies him to the shade;
The lowing herd unto the rivers stray,
Or, panting, seek far off a fresher glade;
The sheep lie close—the lambs forget to play.
Now one wide blaze of heat beams all around;
No zephry stirs the air, no breezes blow.   10
The traveller faint, with eyes that seek the ground,
Moves on his course, irresolute and slow;
And every living thing, by heat opprest,
Seeks some cool cover for a place of rest.

48

Travelling the Prairie in Summer

Now, fierce as Afric's sun, the sultry rage
Of summer beams refulgent overhead,
Striking with ray direct the parched earth,
Till the wide prairie smokes an arid waste,
Brown as in autumn's sad and fading scene.
And the worn trav'ler, spent with the day's warm toil,
Seeks, but in vain, the cool refreshing stream,
Whilst far he wanders from his destined course;
But now the sun declines into the West,
And, as the shades of even round him close,   10
And the cool breeze upon his temples play[s],
With firmer step pursues his long and weary way.

49

Sonnet:
Written during the Late Stormy Weather

Wide o'er the plain the wat'ry powers descend,
And all the gods that rule the upper air,
Wind, rain and thunder, heav'n's dark concave rend,
Whilst the fierce lightnings on pale mortals glare.
Ah, woe the traveller who [is] now abroad,
And o'er the boundless prairie speeds his way,
Tired by hard travail, by his fears o'er aw'd,
How longs he for the glad return of day!
Oh, ye who in warm cabins and at home
Look out upon the night without a sigh,   10
Who, bless'd with comfort, have no need to roam,
Think on the houseless wretch that wanders by;
Nor grudge him what ye can so well afford—
A supper, a warm bed, and pleasant word.

50

A Night on the Prairie

[Preface by the editor of the *Sangamo Journal*] Our old corre-
spondent "H." informs us that he is "not yet defunct," but is still
"in search of adventures" somewhere in the North Western Terri-
tory. The poet found himself in rather an awkward predicament
while on his way up the Mississippi river. "One night," says he, "I
left the boat a little before sun-down at a place on the Missouri
shore. I soon lost my way, *was pursued by wolves and passed the
night in a tree*— when the morning dawned, I got down from my
singular lodging, where, however, as the weather was warm, I
passed the night more comfortably than could be expected.
Messrs. les loups left me a little before sun-rising, and after break-
ing my way through thickets of close briars, I at last found my way
to the river, from which I had strolled about seven miles." The
position of the poet in the tree—the barking of "les loups" while
eying their anticipated "banquet"—and the mutual grimaces of
the parties—would have been worth seeing. The following is said
"to record a literal fact."

O! que je fus dans ma cabanne.

—Thus did the old man say,
"O! were I in my cabin in the wood."
There would we rest and sleep the night away,
Cheer'd by the blaze and plenty of good food;
For I have plenty in my humble home,
Such as the huntsman loves; and were we there,
Thou shouldst partake my bed and my good ven'son share.
But here, alas! upon this lonely plain,
No food to cheer us, and no fire to warm,
We must, per force, lie down 'til sol again   10
Shews his bright face, and all our fears disarm.
And thus, we stretch'd us in the barren wild;
Above, the stars shot forth a feeble ray.
No sleep the weary hours beguil'd;
We rose at early dawn, and wended on our way.

51

Sonnet

The Whip-poor-will
Sung pensively on every tree;
And straight I fell into a reverie.
Moore

O thou shrill warbler of the woody wild,
That plaintively proclaims the close of day,
How oft, in other scenes, thy song beguiled,
And cheer'd at night the long and lonely way!
And first, where Schuylkill's pleasant banks appear,
Near the famed city, I have heard thy note,
To where the Hudson pours his waters clear,
Or great Saint Lawrence flows thro' lands remote.
Or farther yet, by Mississippi's strand,
Where the fierce Saukie roams, its dusky lord,   10
As late I sojourn'd that romantic land—
There have I heard thee, with the wolf abroad.
But wheresoe'er my wandering feet have prest,
Still in sweet Sangamo thou pleas't me best.

Short Philosophical Lyrics

52

Sonnet

In una selva oscura incontrai pastorella.

Again upon these wilds—my weary feet,
From Mississippi's farthest, fairest strand,
Seek the green sward, in other days so sweet,
When first I rambled here, a *stranger* in the land.
How chang'd the scene! late winter's pallid shroud
Wrapp'd the brown plain, that now so bright appears;
Nature, in grief, look'd mournful all around
Where now the vi'let blooms, and Spring her beauty
    wears.
O! that the mind could like the season change,
And cheerful thoughts fill all my soul with green;   10
Then would I, joyful, o'er the landscape range
With a light heart and careless brow serene.
But that can never be!—I hate fine speeches!
How can my heart be glad? The wolves have got my
    breeches!

53

Sonnet

From southern shores to Sangamo I come—
Fair Sangamo, that whilom was my home;
But now, alas! how chang'd does all appear,
Wrapp'd in the livery of the dying year!
The pale inhabitants like ghosts stalk by,
With downcast looks and sad despairing eye.
Sickness their home invades, while each dark hour
Tells of some death, and the destroyer's power.
So dies proud man, and like the leaves that fall
When wintry winds shake the weak branches old,   10
We pass away—the common lot of all—
To add unto the heaps of dead untold.
Sad thought, that man is only born to die,
And perish like the leaves that in our pathway lie.

54

Sonnet

Volti sciolti e pensier' stretti.
Italian Proverb

While, with a seeming gaiety, I tread
These green savannahs of the western wild,
I hear a voice, like echoes from the dead,
Crying aloud, "O, thou of thought beguil'd!
Wilt thou still onward in thy mad career,
Heedless, alike, of warning and of wail;
And, while the wings of death are flapping near,
Wilt thou not listen to the passing gale?
Lo! from the woods around, the solemn knell,
Borne o'er these boundless plains, so sad and lone,   10
Of havoc and dark pestilence doth tell,
While startles on the ear the sudden groan.
Thy face of smiles is but the lights that shew,
More darkly sad, the heart's dim depths below."

55

Sonnet

Though in a wayward mood, at times I stray
Thro' earth's fair beauties, heedless of the charm
That once made happy e'en the darkest day,
While youth bedeck'd the scene with colors warm.
What, tho' no more thro' fancy's glass I see,
Or look on Nature with a poet's eye,
Still can I gaze with fond complacency
On all her charms that yet unequall'd vie.
And who that has a mind, a thinking soul,
Can view those orbs that shine above him here,   10
Nor pause and wonder wherefore do they roll,
And if he's destined for their brighter sphere.
Shall he, when life's poor fluttering dream is past,
Range their bright field and rest in heav'n at last?

56

Astrology Fallacious

In vain we turn our thoughts unto the skies,
And from the stars deduce vain auguries;
They nothing tell us, for they nothing know
Of man—or good, or ill—his joy or woe!
Too far above us, gloriously they shine,
And to the night impart an air divine;
But coldly all look down upon the scene
Of man's low cares, as if he ne'er had been.
And were he not, still, from her bright career,
The moon would shine and bless our hemisphere.   10

57

Written Near Springfield Church-yard

How quiet sleep the dead! How calm are they!
They fear no ills—this mortal coil is done.
The morn awakes them not, to toil a prey,
To shiver in the cold, or faint beneath the sun.
'Tis here in genial spring, when grass is green,
And first the vi'let peeps within the wood,
Invited by the soft and gentle scene,
I sometimes wander in a pensive mood.
The dead are happy! Yet it seemeth strange,
When Nature smiles around without alloy,   10
That they no more the flow'ry fields may range
And start again to life, and all its joy.
Yet so it is—the dead return no more.
Forever silent, here they still remain.
No wandering ghost from Pluto's gloomy shore
Ever returned to say, "we come again."

58

Sonnet

We all must tread the downward way.
Horace

This vapor we call life is but a breath,
A point, a shadow merely. Do not say
We live—for lo! and in a moment, Death,
On his black pinions, hurries us away.
Alas! and must we leave the glorious day,
And all we love, and in a grave be laid?
Ask yon pale corse—remove that coffin lid—
He answers not—for nothing can it say.
And is this all—that nothing we can know?
Perplexing doubt! O vain inquiry made!   10
Is no one wise enough? No! none below,
However wise, can penetrate the shade.
Dim mists, and dark impenetrable gloom
Forever shroud this secret of the tomb.

59

L'envoy

In una selva oscura incontrai pastorella.

Erewhile, o'ertaken by the night, I stray[ed]
Thro' a dark wood, where the dim, dubious way
I could not trace—but in a doubtful mood,
Like one that's lost, sad, sore perplex'd I stood.
When lo! a shepherd glided to my side,
Like a good angel, come to be my guide.
Bright were his locks and most benign his air,
Who ask'd me how I came to wander there.
"This wood," says he, "bears doubting Error's name,
Nor enter'd yet who safely from it came.   10
But see yon star!" He pointed to the sight
Which, all dissolv'd away, had vanish'd quite;
And in its stead shone forth the morning light.
"You doubted," said my guide. "The path most clear
To you was dark—so ever must appear
To him who trusts alone to Reason here."

60

Spirits

While late I sit, lone musing by the fire,
The mem'ry of past days will dimly rise.
Sadly around, meanwhile, the night wind sighs,
And, one by one, the embers slow expire.
What sound was that, which on the ear of night
Breaks the dead silence of the midnight hour?
The wind, perchance, or else some wand'ring sprite
Releas'd awhile to breathe in upper air.
They say, at certain times, without control,
The buried dead at this dark watch appear;   10
A sudden horror tells their presence near,
With shrieks upon the gale that chill the soul—
Such was the sound which late the night winds bore,
Like some poor wretch thrown bleeding on the shore.

61

Sonnet

Sad o'er my spirit rise the tender shades
Of other days and other scenes long fled;
And as their presence all my soul pervades,
I seem to hold communion with the dead.
Dim, misty forms—they hover round my bed,
And interpose between the moon and me,
While solemn music, breathing overhead,
With grief and joy is mix'd alternately.
"And do ye live, dear shades," I joyful cry—
"And is it then an idle tale they tell   10
Who said ye were not? Wherefore do ye fly,
And cheat my fond embrace? alas! farewell!"
Like the thin mist of morn they melt away,
Whilst rises in the East the god of day.

62

The Hindoo Heaven

There is, as I have read in Sanscrit lore,
A happy island where the bless'd remain;
Fann'd by celestial gales, the blissful shore
Forever shields them from disease and pain.
There in immortal bowers, with roses crown'd,
They feast, they sing, they while the hours away;
The sweetest odors are diffus'd around,
And no dark night succeeds to glorious day.
Kama looks down upon the blessed scene,
And Siraswatta with the golden hair   10
(A goddess born—among the gods most fair,
Supreme in beauty) is their radiant queen.
Yet ere a mortal can her love attain,
On Siva's altars he must first be slain.

63

The Improvement of Modern Times

Tempora mutantur

Now, for a thousand years, the world has lain
In deepest ignorance and mental night;
At length breaks forth the cheerful light,
And mind resumes her long disputed reign.
Fell superstition, by the vapors fed,
Engender'd in the dark abyss of time;
The morning sun far hence hath sped,
And Science takes her onward march sublime.
The dreams of ignorance no more prevail;
The monk is gone, the convent low is laid,   10
And all their nonsense but the idle tale
Of some old crone still ling'ring in the shade.
The nations now a brighter vigil keep,
And stand erect, like giants rous'd from sleep.

64

Le Solitaire

En ce coin je me porte bien
Sans rat, sans chat, sans chien.

In these dark days when gloomy winter reigns,
And all without looks comfortless and cold,
How happy he who, by his own fireside,
Finds all he wants, nor idly asks for more.
Yet some will say, "How sad to sit alone,
Without a mate, or prattling children near.
Sure such a life can never happy be,
So still, so dull—void of all companie."
But I, who am of philosophic mood,
And care but little for the idle crowd,   10
With mine own tho'ts can while the hours away,
Best pleas'd when most alone and neither sad nor gay.

65

Sonnet

Piu lune gia, quand' i'jeci 'l mal sonna,
Che del futuro mi squarcia 'l velame.
Dante

How like myself in former years and now;
Yet how unlike, my fortune still the same.
The scene alone is chang'd; still on my brow
Rests the dead calm that hides a soul all flame.
Musing, yet restless; thoughtful, yet not wise;
Ling'ring, yet onward still, my steps pursue
A phantom shapeless, that deludes these eyes,
Which if I follow not doth still pursue.
What have I gain'd in all this waste of years—
(Many strange lands, and stranger men I've seen)   10
Th' amount summ'd up, what is it? tears, sad tears.
The harvest of my hopes, what hath it been?
To gather thorns where I expected flowers,
And in life's lowest scene consume the hours.

66

Sonnet

Little avails it that the mind would be
Firm, independent, if our outward state
Shew the frail ensigns of sad penury,
For such the vulgar shun—or low, or great.
And he who dares to give his mind full scope
Will find ere long, by Folly held in scorn,
How small the chance, how slender is the hope,
Against such odds to urge his way forlorn.
Success, not merit, is the passport here—
This, this alone, the vulgar herd can sway;   10
Only succeed—thou hast no more to fear—
No matter how, so that thou win'st the day;
Leave all thou lov'st; be thou a friend to none—
And be a villain? aye, the field is won!

67

Content the Best Fortune

The soul that's ever restless and abroad
Will never know what peace and quiet mean.
If we'd be happy, seek the narrow road
That leads into Obscurity's dim vale.
There dwells the Matron, holy, chaste and pure,
Truth by her side and Meekness looking low,
Whose ear the world's loud noises can't endure,
Averse to empty pride and vulgar show.
Why do we wander into climes remote
When all of worth at home may best be found?   10
The shepherd lives more happy in his cot
Then he who travels all the world around.
Most learning is mere pedantry and pride—
Not wisest he who yet the most doth know.
Me let the Muses innocently guide,
Unknown alike to fame, to want and woe.
I would not be the buzz of all mankind,
The hapless idol of the crowd insane—
Toss'd to and fro with every idle wind—
Giddy with loud applauses, false as vain.   20
But let me live within some quiet nook
The happy life that best the muses love,
And when I die there find a peaceful grave,
Where sighing winds are heard and gentler waters lave.

68

Truth

Le vron seul est beau; le vrai seul est simable.
Boileau

The days are past when idle dreams could please,
And vain imaginings would give me ease.
Now other thoughts employ the anxious mind,
And more important far, if less refined.
No air-born hopes dance thro' my giddy brain—
Life's weak illusions—and its constant pain.
These for a while, like opiates, may relieve
The sickly soul, but will at last deceive.
'Tis sweet to dwell in pleasure's painted bowers,
And fancy all the bliss that might be ours;   10
But never yet did real contentment flow
From such a source, or mitigate our woe.
'Tis truth alone can fortify the mind,
And make us to the ills of fate resigned.
Boldly to know the truth, the truth to brave—
This frees us from the coward and the slave.
Look danger in the face; there's nought to fear.
At distance great, it vanishes more near.
Not always happy whom no cares molest,
But he who can support those cares the best.   20

69

Sonnet

To struggle on, to struggle on for aye—
This seems of man th' inexorable doom.
And yet how quickly glides his life away—
No rest between the cradle and the tomb.
In youth, too eager and with spirits light,
We still anticipate a brighter sphere,
Filling the mind with fancies all too bright,
And revel in the visions insincere.
Yet in the real can only truth be found.
When sad experience lifts the veil between,   10
No longer then we tread on fairy ground,
But view with sober eye the common scene.
Plain truth alone and unadorned we see,
Life's vulgar prose and stern reality.

Poems on Legend and Mythology

70

Taur Arthur

The old grey stone, the old grey stone,
Where I have sat for hours alone
And look'd upon the flowers of spring,
And heard the breezes whispering!
Now sad I sit for hours alone,
But not upon the old grey stone.
Again I feel the genial spring—
Again the breeze is whispering;
But here no flowers around are seen,
Nor Nature's soul reviving green;   10
But all is sad and wild and lone,
Like winter near the old grey stone.
    The old grey stone, the old grey stone,
When last I wander'd there alone,
I look'd upon the stormy sea
And hail'd a form exultingly—
For in her skiff, my Lela's hair
And bosom to the storm lay bare,
While fearless to the shore she sprung,
And deftly to my side she clung.   20
    Alas! while here I wander wide,
I see no Lela by my side;
And stretching o'er the plain my eye,
Nought but the level waste descry,
While black the coming tempests sweep,
Like those upon the restless deep,
As sad I wander forth alone
And muse upon the old grey stone.
    Alas! what fickle things are we!
Between us rolls the roaring sea,   30
And we may never meet again
Where the grey Tor frowns on the main,
Nor gather flowers along the lea,

Nor look upon the tossing sea.
And yet that solitary scene
Appears as fresh before mine eyen
As if it were but yesterday
I dash'd aside the foaming spray
And stood upon that ancient strand,
The Briton's own unconquer'd land,   40
Where he the Dane and Saxon slew,
And gave them to the wild sea-mew;
Where Arthur fell, and Britain too—
All, save that lone and sea-bent shore
Where the dark waves incessant roar—
Where still the sons of Arthur keep,
And where they still defy the deep.
    Land of the cairn and cavern rude,
The Cymri's ancient solitude!
Though I may wander far from thee,   50
In worlds beyond the distant sea—
Caradoch's son—I still am free!
And still, a spark of British fire
I breathe along the trembling lyre;
Though faint, indeed, and all constrain'd
To that Talliessen erst maintain'd,
When fiercely to his warriors round
He bade the thund'ring chords resound,
But dash'd them by and seized the spear
When Dane or Saxon foe were near,   60
Nor would awake the chords again
Until the northern foe were slain.
Then with wild ardor rose the note
That with the Cymri's accents spoke.
And still are heard the witching rhymes
That tell the deeds of other times,
And still, they say, at even lone
The bard is at the old grey stone,
Or round Tintaggel vigil keeps,
Where Arthur, with his Britons, sleeps.   70
At close of day the forms are seen

Careering o'er the moon-lit green,
What time, releas'd from fairie land,
They seek again the Cornish strand,
And couch the spear, or bend the bow,
That lays the traitor Modred low.
    Such vision sees the country maid,
As late she trips it o'er the glade—
And these the tales my youth beguil'd,
Told by my mother when a child,   80
As, many a wintry eve alone,
We'd talk about the old grey stone.

71

The Hall of Odin

In Odin's hall the feast was spread,
And fast the mantling goblet sped—
When, like the flash of heaven, came
A spirit from the fields of fame.
The warriors rise—with one accord
Forth from its scabbard leaps the sword.
And striking each his dinted shield
Due honors to the hero yield.
"Welcome to Odin's hall," they cry;
"The feast is spread, the ale foams high,　　　　　　10
And the sweet song which Odin loves
Awaits you in the blest abodes."
With joy he takes the honor'd seat
While clanging arms the hero greet.
Huge cauldrons hold the warlike cheer—
Three savage bulls, nine fallow deer—
And in the midst a mighty bowl,
Whence drinks his fill each thirsty soul.
With haste they seize the welcome food,
The giant's prey from Lorna's wood;　　　　　　20
Then from the skulls of foemen quaff
The northern wine, and grimly laugh.
And while they thus the hours employ,
Thelma awakes the chords of joy.
He sang of Modred's bloody fight,
Where cowered the raven's fearful might,
And of the choosers of the slain,
Who haunt the fatal battle plain
And in Valhalla to the brave
Hand round the bowl that heroes crave—　　　　　　30
Valkiri, fearful in the fight,
Immortal here in beauty bright.
How Odin sought the shades below,

Balder's avenging hour to know,
And woke the prophetess to tell
The dark decrees of heaven and hell.
Of Thor, the hunter of the wild,
And how the giants were beguiled.
These had Thor's mighty hammer got,
And sore he grieved his hapless lot;   40
But Lok, whose deep deceptive brain
Ascendence with the gods could gain,
O'er Thor's swart visage threw a veil,
With silken robes to hide his mail,
And gaily then led forth the fair
Adorn'd with bridal jewels rare.
To Jotunheim their course they wend,
And soon the giants' hold is gained.
Much wonder'd they at maid so tall,
And her broad shoulders more than all.   50
Her beauty so the giants took
That they beneath the veil must look,
And more and more the giants stare
When her fierce eye-balls on them glare;
But Thor his mighty hammer gains
And dashes out the giants' brains.
Fraught was the song with northern lore
That now another burthen bore.
He sang of Thrym and Lodbrog strong,
The Danish chief and pride of song;   60
The serpent, that by Midgard's steep
Appears upheaving from the deep,
And on his scaley folds displays
The sea's green hues and sunny rays.
Him shun the daring sons of Niord,
Nor venture in their skiffs abroad—
Or seen to Hela's dark domain
They sink beneath the rolling main.
Then sung the scald that fatal day
When all the gods must pass away,   70
And come that last and final hour

The wolf shall the bright sun devour,
And Hela will require the slain
From every distant battle plain.
But at the last shall Fenris dire
Beneath Thor's iron mace expire,
And Sinna back again receive
The monstrous birth she erst did give;
And then another world will rise,
With greener fields and brighter skies.   80
Well pleased, they listen to the strains,
But small belief the minstrel gains;
Fear touches not these warlike souls,
But all believe in draining bowls.
Lok urged the foaming goblet round,
But dash'd his own upon the ground.
Then deep they drink—their shouts invade
Nifflema's dark and dreary shade.
Their wild debauch they long maintain,
And thrice the mighty bowl they drain.   90
Fierce ardours in their bosoms glow;
They seize the spear, they bend the bow.
Each warrior boasts his deeds of yore,
Then sighs to think he fights no more.
Gigantic Fulma hurls his spear
That wounds unhurt the empty air;
And dreaming still of war's alarms,
Thorlar and Orfar rise in arms.
Stern from the seats of grey renown
Three aged chiefs rush fiercely down: 100
Orcar and Thorsi, known of eld—
First in the ranks of battle held—
With horrid Thoscar's giant form
Raging like a northern storm.
In haste he grasps his sword of might
And rushes headlong to the fight.
Thin Cothon saw, and seeing, sped
A javelin at the giant's head;
When Orcar, Scandia's savage lord,

Opposed his helm and buckler broad.   110
But for a while is fate delayed;
He falls at last by Thorsi's blade.
Three gaping wounds his soul let forth
To wander in the frozen North.
Like waves that lash cold Norway's shore,
So loud is heard the wild uproar
The dead awaken at the sound,
And the pale spectres flit around—
When Odin's voice in thunder came,
And quench'd, at once, the martial flame.   120
    Their arms are prostrate laid.
    Freia appears amid the host—
    The din of war in joy is lost—
    And all admire the maid.
Like the bright moon in wintry streams,
So Freia's face with beauty beams.
She moves a queen in Odin's hall,
And leads each captive heart in thrall.

Notes

Odin, Oden, or Woden the Thunderer, was worshipped as a god
by the Saxons. He is supposed to have been a great leader among
his countrymen and very successful in war. Odin was said to im-
part the gift of verse, and hence the phrase, "Odin's gift," so fre-
quent in runic rhyme.

Valhalla, or the Hall of Odin, was the northern heaven, where
the souls of departed heroes enjoyed the pleasures of the ban-
quet, drinking ale and mead out of the skulls of their fallen
enemies.

The Raven was the standard of the Danes, woven with magic
spells. And they looked up to it as it flapped in the wind as a cer-
tain signal of victory or defeat.

The Valkiri, or Choosers of the slain, answer to the Fates or
Fatal Sisters of the ancients.

The Descent of Odin, and the awakening of the Prophetess from her death-like trance, are finely told in a poem by the poet Gray:

> Thrice he traced the runic rhyme,
> Thrice pronounced with accents dread
> The thrilling verse that wakes the dead.

Thor was the son of Odin and is represented as armed with a terrible mace, or hammer of huge size.

Lok is an evil god. He assisted Thor in the destruction of the giants. He was remarkable for his cunning and played many Yankee tricks among the gods.

Thrym was an ancient king, and this is all I know about him. He is thus introduced in a poem translated by Heber:

> High on a mound, in haughty state,
> Thrym the King of the Thursi sate;
> For his dogs he was twisting collars of gold
> And trimming the manes of his coursers bold.

Lodbrog, or Lodbrog with the hairy breeches, as he is usually denominated, was either a Danish or Norwegian warrior, remarkable for his valor and great strength.

The Serpent of Midgard makes a great figure in the *Edda,* an ancient poem written in the Icelandic tongue and containing almost all we know of the superstitious belief of the former inhabitants of the north of Europe.

Neord was the Neptune of the North.

Hela, or Death.

Scald among the Scandanavians answered to the Bhardh of the Britons; and, like the Bard, he was a prophet as well as poet. The words implying in both languages a foreteller of future events. They were the primitive priests, and were held in great veneration by their countrymen who, however, took the liberty of believing just as much of their predictions as suited them best. They accompanied the warriors to the field, and urged them on to deeds of desperate valor by their rude rhymes, the same as the small-beer poets may be supposed to have done in the late war with the predatory Sacs and Foxes.

Sinna was the consort of Lok; between them they begot Hela or Death. The wolf, Fenris, and the Serpent of Midgard were also of their manufacture.

At the Twilight of the Gods, as it is finely expressed in the *Edda,* Fenris will eat up the sun, but Thor will destroy both the wolf and the Serpent of Midgard. The gods themselves will finally pass away, and a new world arise—better, of course, than the old one.

Nifflemir, or the northern hell, is cold—where the souls of cowards, and those who die in any way but in battle, wander about in a kind of dim twilight.

Friega, or Freia, was the consort of Odin, and the northern Venus.

72

The Gods of Old

As yet all shapeless lay the dark dim Thought,
Inert, inactive, in the womb of night,
Until with life elate, to being brought,
It starts from chaos, living, warm and bright.
Thus rose the gods, faith of the elder times,
Ere man attain'd his prime, and green the earth,
The progeny divine of those bright climes
Where still Apollo reigns and where the Muse had birth:
Osiris, Isis, worshipped on the Nile;
Inds' swarming deities, a countless train;   10
Prolific issue of great Brama's mind,
With all that rule the Tartars' rugged plain.
But other deities the Norsemen sway,
Whose iron rule their stormy chiefs obey:
Oden and Woden and the giant Thor—
Rude Saxon gods were these, and famed in fight,
Their sole employment waging bloody war,
The clang of arms and carnage their delight.
Valhalla was their heaven, where they swill
Prodigious bowls of mead and humming ale;   20
But even here, the poet's voice could still
Their headlong rage, and over arms prevail.
Grim smiled the warriors when the poet sung—
Not Freya's face could charm them more
(Immortal Freya, Odin's matchless queen)—
Valhalla's echoing halls the sounds prolong;
Hela was pleas'd, and Fenris ceas'd to roar.
Thus, by Imagination's aid,
The gods of olden time were made.
'Twas then the poet stood elate,   30
Erect of port and high in state;
And kings put off a mortal crown
The Muse's laurel wreath to own.

But in these vile degenerate days
There's few that give the poet praise,
While each dull knave in duller prose can shine,
And cant and nonsense now are hail'd divine.

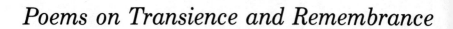

Poems on Transience and Remembrance

73

Song

Ah, me! when I remember
    The days of youth long past,
I feel like chill December,
    Whose clouds are o'er me cast.

In gentle youth we fondly dream,
    And deck the path with flowers,
But coming years a light will beam
    That spoils this heaven of ours.

When young the pulse will beat,
    And beauty fire the soul,   10
But old—is quench'd the heat
    Which once own'd no control.

Yet, if with youth we lose the joy,
    We lose our sorrow too;
Then what availeth here to sigh,
    Since nothing is more true!

The night, however long, is past—
So sorrow is forgot at last;
    And if our joys are all too brief,
    Just, just as lasting is our grief;   20
Nothing is constant here below;
Joys flee away, and tears forget to flow.

74

The Roses

in se mal vivo,
E morto in lei ch' e morta.
Tasso

The scenes of youth I've wander'd o'er,
And ev'ry spot belov'd of yore—
But, ah! how chang'd doth each appear,
And wither'd, all that once was dear!
Where are the fields, the flow'rs fled,
The sky that nature canopied—
That deep-blue sky, to fancy bright
With ev'ry form of love and light?
Are these the fields, are these the flowers
That charm'd me in life's morning hours?   10
Are these the friends that once I knew,
Belov'd, free-hearted, kind and true?
Dear friends! one with a cold disdain,
Saluted, scorns to speak again;
Another, but not quite so high,
Just gives a nod, then passes by!
Alas! not only these, but thou,
Great Nature, wear'st an alter'd brow!
The fields are green, yet to my view
They wear the pallid winter's hue;   20
Still bloom the flow'rs, but to my sight,
Or smell, they yield no sweet delight.
Tho' like a seraph's voice, the sound
Of gentle zephyrs breathe around—
Like hollow blasts they seem to sigh,
And moaning, tell of days gone by!
Not so, when the fair Eleanour
Vouchsaf'd me for her paramour;
And gather'd from their yielding stem

Two roses, worth a diadem—   30
And gazing at the flowers awhile,
On them, and me, did faintly smile.
"These are an emblem meet," she said,
"Of what befalls full many a maid;
They bloom awhile in life's warm June,
But then, alas! they fade as soon."
Like them, she blush'd upon my view;
Like them, alas! she faded too!
Fair moralist! thy words were sooth,
For thou, too, perish'd in thy youth,   40
And like the flow'r thou lov'dst so well,
Thus sweetly bloom'd, thus early fell.
        In vain may other roses bloom;
They only deck the fair one's tomb.
In vain the sky looks down serene;
I turn me, mourning, from the scene,
Or gath'ring one sweet flow'ret, shed
Its odours o'er the lovely dead.
Then ask my heart if this can be,
Or is it not all phantasy—   50
A wild'ring dream from fancy sprung,
Or some sad tale by poet sung?

75

Lines

Con un sospiro mi rimembro.
Petrarch

Dark o'er my brow the vanished years
    (When hope was high and life was new)
Flit dimly by, all paled with tears,
    And for a while the past renew.

The forms of other days I see,
    The gay, the fair, the brave, the true;
And one, alas! how fair was she
    That sleeps beneath the mourning yew.

And still can mem'ry fondly trace
    The rural scene where last we met,   10
Where art so well did nature grace—
    Ah, those sweet flow'rs, I see them yet!

Calm, gentle Thames before us lay,
    Smiling serene, as infants smile;
And many a skiff, with pennon gay,
    Glided unheeded by the while.

Th' enamour'd breeze upon her cheek
    Dash'd the rich clusters of her hair,
Brown auburn locks that lovers seek,
    And strew'd them o'er her bosom fair.   20

And there with fond, admiring eyes,
    While seated on a grassy mound,
She'd listen to the plaintive cries
    Of tender lambs that sported round,

Or pluck the young and opening flowers
    That by her side profusely lay—
Another Eve in Eden's bowers;
    As fair, and innocent, as they.

76

Lines

When I recall the days gone by,
Remembrance prompts the frequent sigh,
    And tears, unbidden, flow.
Alas! to think on joys that were
But adds unto our present care,
    And more augments the woe.

Then, since the past affords no joy,
Let mirth the present hour employ—
    Why always look so sad?
The past is but a dream that's flown;   10
The present only is our own—
    Then, while it's ours, be glad.

What boots it now, poor heart, to tell
Or think of her thou lov'dst so well—
    That fervid dream is past!
Hadst thou thy all of hope attained,
Ere this the goblet had been drain'd—
    It could not always last!

Whate'er the joy, it would have flown;
But still the present is our own.   20
    Then why at fate repine?
I care not for the fair, for she
Is old and loveless grown, like me—
    Nor longer is divine!

But I can still, like Hafez, smile,
And all the weary hours beguile
    Like that sweet poet gay.
I climb the muses' sacred hill,

And visions bright my fancies fill,
    With many a charming lay.   30

The poet's heart is ever young—
This long ago the Persian sung,
    And quaff'd the rosy wine;
And though, at times, the bard would sigh
His sorrow, it was never dry—
    Let Hafez's fate be mine!

77

Lines

How speed our lives away—
A few brief moments and they're gone for aye!
A breath, a bubble—how they speed away!
Thus sung the bard of old;
Thus sighs the modern lay.
Thus ages are by moments told—
The same a thousand years, as if but yesterday!
Yet Nature, ever young,
With liberal hand hath flung
E'en now, as at her early birth,   10
Upon this fair, propitious earth,
A charm, a beauty of undying worth.
Ten thousand years ago
The rose was young and smelt as sweet as now,
And still, the queen of flowers
Gladdens our halls and bowers!
Unchanging Nature, old, yet ever new,
Still bends the sky of blue.
Lovely the landscape smiles as it was used to do.
All die, yet all remain—   20
Though changing, still the same,
A link-unbroken, never-ending chain.
And still, ten thousand years from hence,
Boon Nature will her gifts dispense,
The seasons roll as heretofore,
And the rich harvest of the field
To man a liberal bounty yield—
The sun will bless his path, and morn and night restore.

78

Many Years Ago

Gentle maiden, gentle maiden,
    With a voice soft and low,
You remind me, you remind me,
    Of years long ago.

And the river where we stand,
    And the waters as they flow,
They remind me, they remind me,
    Of years long ago.

Like thee was Lela fair,
    With a voice soft and low,   10
As we stood by the river's side
    Many years ago.

But that river was the Thames
    And this the Sangamo,
Nor are you the Lela fair
    I lov'd long ago.

You are fair, you are fair,
    On your cheeks the roses glow,
But you are not the fair maid
    I lov'd long ago.   20

79

From the Italian

In ma scha cocura incontrai pastorella.
Filicaia

Lone wandering at night,
I sought that ancient tree
Where, once a happy wight,
I was wont to meet with thee.

But when I found thee not,
My troubled heart was sore,
And returning to my cot,
I vow'd to love no more.

But we cannot soon forget
The one we lov'd so well,   10
And still with fond regret
My sad looks the tale will tell.

80

My Native Land

My native land, my native land,
O, were I in my native land!
This cheek so wan, this brow so pale
Would tell another, joyful tale,
And light my spirit be, and bland,
Were I but in my native land.
Ah, me! what many weary lengths I've past
Since I on England look'd my last,
And turn'd these aching eyes away
From those belov'd thro' many a day,   10
And saw the land fade on the deep,
Nor could for very sadness weep.
And yet, 'tis fair where I have been,
With mighty hills and vales between;
The rivers roll, like oceans wide,
And forests spread on every side;
The fields are bright with waving grain,
While brighter flowers adorn the plain.
But can such scenes my cares beguile,
Or wean me from my own green isle?   20
Ah, no! my heart responsive sighs,
No other lands, no other skies,
Can win from me a willing smile,
Or tear me from my native isle.
O, there the gentlest breezes play,
And Nature smiles serenely gay;
There health is breath'd in every gale,
A sweeter smell the flowers exhale,
And hearts are kind, with nought of guile,
In that dear land, my native isle.   30

81

The Exile

O, far away! O, far away!
When far away I roam,
Where'er my wand'ring feet may stray,
My thoughts are still at home.

Along the Mohawk's pleasant stream,
Or in Canadian woods forlorn,
Where scarce the sun can point a beam
Or penetrate the morn.

By Niagara's giant falls,
Where deaf'ning waters roar,   10
Or deep Ontario, vex'd by squalls,
My weary course explore.

Or, farther, in the distant West,
Along the prairies green,
Where scarce the foot of man hath press'd
Or trace of him is seen.

Whether by flood or field I stray,
By wood or mountain side,
In melancholy mood, or gay,
My thoughts at home abide.   20

82

The Wish

Long years have fled since first I left my home
In far off England, where I first drew breath;
But never yet, wherever I might roam,
Have I seen ought I'd wish to see again.
And when the grisly phantom, pallid Death,
Knocks at the door of this clay tenement,
My only wish shall be (to ease the pain)
That in mine own green isle these weary bones be lain.

83

Sonnet

Oft in fond dreams I view my native land,
And see the friends that I was wont to see;
There once again I join the social band,
In concert sweet and rare felicity.
But as the morning breaks in sober grey
Along the waste of Sangamo's dull scene,
Floats the light visions of the night away,
Like scatter'd mist upon the prairie green.
Still, as the evening shades again descend,
Again in that sweet land of dreams I stray;   10
Again I walk the fields with many a friend;
Again the landscape smiles serenely gay.
Thus half my cares I can at night beguile,
And dream myself again in Britain's isle.

84

A Sonnet

Though I am distant from my native land,
And all my years have pass'd in Folly's maze,
Still do I love, upon this foreign strand,
To cheer my mind with hopes of better days.
Ah! what avails it to recall the past,
When all it brings is but remember'd pain?
Youth spent in trifles, manhood ebbing fast
Too plainly tell me every hope is vain!
And what is life, that we so fondly crave?
In youth a torment—curse in after years—
A path that leads forever to the grave,
Whether in joy pursued, or else in tears.
Like bubbles o'er the lake we pass away;
The longest but a moment here can stay.

10

85

L'etourdi

When I think on all I've seen,
What I've suffer'd, where have been,
Then I'm apt to cry, "Heigh, O!"
Sighing sad, where'er I go.
But never long in sorrow's cell
Gloomy grief with me can dwell;
For if a sigh my heart betray,
Mirth soon chases it away.
Thus alternate grief and joy,
Turn by turn, my hours employ;   10
Sighing sad, or laughing gay,
Life with me's an April day.

86

Secret Sorrow

To sit in silence and to muse
On all the past is sorrow still,
And fain would my poor heart refuse
This constant monitor of ill.

Therefore I strive, amid the crowd,
To wear a face of mickle glee,
But vain the task, however loud
The laugh or idle jest may be.

Then deem not, though I seem so gay,
Without a latent trace of ill,   10
For mostly then my looks betray—
When gayest I am saddest still.

The cause of this is easy shown:
We would not that our thoughts be known.
Experience teaches us, and pride,
The sorrows of the heart to hide.

Two Lyrics on the Black Hawk War

87

On the Second Arming against Black Hawk

    The cry is heard once more:
"To arms, to arms, to arms!"
From Mississippi's shore
Are heard the wild alarms.
The Sauks are for the fight—
Or whether wrong, or right,
They will the land maintain.
"We will not leave," they cry,
"Where our forefathers lie—
But here we'll die!"   10
"Behold our lands, how wide
On either ocean's side
From sun to sun they lay.
Our blankets now
Can cover all we have.
Tomanoc, and they grudge
The scanty boon we crave.
Cold and hard-hearted they—
The pale-face hems us round—
For us no sympathy.   20
They drive us from the ground.
Behold our destiny:
To starve, or fight, or flee.
The winter's biting frost
Was hard upon our host—
Ye felt the agony
That made e'en warriors weep.
Better in death to sleep
Than hear our children's cry—
And shall we basely fly?"   30
    Thus to his warriors wild
The fierce Atassi spoke,
And their deep vengeance woke.

They curse the white man's guile
That caught them in the toil,
And for a bauble
Their rich lands convey'd.
"And still they're ours," they said;
"We could not sell,
Nor could they buy   40
The land wherein our fathers lie."
Then, like the fiends, their lot lament
When driven into banishment.
A female of the tribe is slain,
And her red blood sinks in the plain;
A baleful fire gleams at night,
A witness of the horrid rite.
Dire shrieks and fearful screams
Disturb the white man' dreams.
With double fears distrest,   50
The mother folds her infant to the breast;
While favor'd by the night's dark screen,
The prowling savage lurks unseen,
And where he makes his bloody lair
Red murder marks his course
And smoking ruins mock
The morning fair.
Alas, how cruel man—
Apply what arts we can—
When left at large   60
The fiery passions sweep,
Fierce, hot as hell,
And like the ocean deep.
As the grim bear in fight,
So wakes the western might.
With the hollow-sounding drum
In lengthen'd files they come.
Tall, stout, and strong, and fair,
Kentucky's sons are there,
Who, like the prairie when on fire,   70
Burn unextinguish'd in their ire,

With many more I cannot name,
But equally the heirs of fame.
    Now, Black Hawk, count your stars aright;
Your braves must nerve them for the fight.
No childrens' play will this be found,
But fight you must, or quit the ground.
Dimly I see the battle form,
Still darkening like a coming storm;
The clang of arms I seem to hear—   80
The twanging bow, the shiver'd spear—
While the quick rifle cracks the air,
And scalping knife my senses scare,
As mixed with shouts, and savage screams,
The combat thickens in my dreams!

    Schetabo! give her one small drink;
My muse already 'gins to swink.
Delightful sounds, the clang of arms,
When we are safe from war's alarms,
But these, our border frays, ill suit   90
The Bard, and strike the Muses mute!
He, like the maids themselves, is coy,
Nor war's rough sports can give him joy.
A mere pretence to courage his,
All vapour born, and goes off—fiss!
And if Nishishin he should see,
Adieu, adieu, to poetry!
Farewell the Muses; then good night.
He dies, and that with sheer affright.
Then do not drag him to the wars;   100
No taste has he for wounds and scars.
He spills no blood, but only ink,
And at the scalping knife would blink.
But though the Bard himself is tame,
He measures out the hero's fame;
And if you do go forth without me,
See what a song I'll make about ye!
Ajax himself, nor him who died,

The mighty Greek, by Ilium's side,
Shall you in deeds of arms outshine.   110
Your praise shall sing the Muses nine,
And to the very heaven of verse
Will I each Sucker's deeds rehearse.
Great Homer's self I will outdo
When my sweet strains shall sing of you;
And I will rear the lofty rhyme
For this, and for all future time,
That ages yet unborn may know
The deeds achiev'd by Sangamo!
Odin's gift across the sea   120
To Sucker land I bear with me,
And still unto the Sucker's praise
I consecrate my sweetest lays.
No other sounds my lyre will own,
Or sad, or grave, or gay the tone.
Swiftly my fingers sweep the strings
When in the Sucker's praise she sings,
But feeble all, and weak the lay,
When from sweet Sangamo I stray.

88

[Untitled Poem on General James D. Henry in the Black Hawk War]

Long did our frontier naked lay,
To savage men a prey.
The Black Hawk hover'd o'er the West
And scar'd the dove of peace from rest.
Night saw the fires ascent,
And awful beam'd the day;
Men, babes, and women fell,
As rose the Indian yell.
Black horror reign'd, and all was gloom around.
The white man fled the battle ground   10
And hasten'd from the fight away.
Where, where was then our stay?
At length a warrior rose
Like lightning on our foe,
Who sought the savage in his den—
And thence escaped again.
He follow'd on the Indian trail
And bade the savage Sac beneath him quail.
But now upon the western plain
Is gentle peace return'd again.   20
The farmer seeks the cabin door,
So lately stained with human gore,
Nor fears the savage Indian yell.
     Brave Henry, foremost in the fight,
To him we owe the meed of might.
The Bard his deeds should tell;
And proud our Sangamo should be
That boasts a warrior such as he!
A braver soul ne'er yet drew breath,
Or battled in the ranks of death.   30
Kind, frank, and free, bold for the right—
A lamb in peace—a lion in the fight.

Miscellaneous Short Lyrics

89

On the Present of a Pincushion by a Lady

Fair leddie, I've your gift receivit,
An' faith, I'm proud, ye may believe it.
The pretty wee thing ye hae sent me,
In vera truth, it should content me;
For when I look upon its border,
An' see the pins set in due order,
I tak' the hint, an' dare opine
Ye mean by them the Muses nine
Thro' a' my heavenly verses shine;
Yet, aiblins, 'tis the ither way,   10
An' these same pins are made to say
That I nine wives maun hae in a',
(Gude Lord, defend us e'en frae twa!)
Or else, nine bairns ye do intend—
Enough to bring me to my end!
But this I canna weal believe,
Nor think poor Bardie thus ye'd grieve—
Therefor' the ither sense I'll take,
And thank you for the Muse's sake.

90

L'amour Coquet

Gentle Chloe was a maid
And of Collin much afraid.
Much afraid, indeed, was she,
Or pretended so to be.
And though she lov'd him passing well,
Her love for him would never tell,
'Till, at last, the pensive swain
Quitted all the rural train.
A farewell to the fields he took,
His bleating fold and shepherd's crook,   10
And in London's busy town,
All his love and sorrow drown.
Then 'twas Chloe's turn to mourn,
And now she sighs for his return.
But soon there came a smiling youth—
A flatt'ring tongue had he, in sooth,
And something else so pleasing to,
That Chloe knew not what to do.
Still her old love for Collin burns,
But this subdues her heart by turns.   20
Ye lovers, read my tale aright!
Nor trust to love when out of sight;
And though our Collin still was true,
Yet, in the end, he married Sue!

91

The Independent Philosopher

Mid hopes and fears,
Mid joys and tears,
    My onward course I go.
Me heedeth not
The world a jot;
    I treat it even so.

So we are quits,
The world and its—
    We care not one for th' other.
The world may pass—   10
The world's an ass—
    Each honest man's my brother.

92

Sonnet

. . . in Spagna, o in Italia pia belle.

There is a charm in foreign lands to be,
And hear the stranger's speech, yet feel at home—
Such as fair Spain, or fairer Italy,
The wild sierra, or the classic dome.
But wand'ring where no trace of man is seen,
Or merely rude and savage, without soul,
In vain the prairie spreads a sea of green,
In vain the mountains tower, the rivers roll.
O let me wander where the moonlight plays
Through orange groves where stately Seville stands,   10
Or where the gondolier and Tasso's lays
Make the heart leap in those romantic lands.
There let me wander—there, at last, repose,
Where grows the myrtle and where blooms the rose.

93

Il Melancolico per Amore

Bella Italia, amate sponde,
Pur vi torno a rivider?
Trema in petto e se confonde
L'alma oppressa dal piacer.
Metastasio

Sweet Italy! and shall I yet return,
Shall I, again, behold sweet Italy?
O, how my bosom burns when thoughts of thee
Come o'er me, in the land where I sojourn!

Well I remember—can I e'er forget—
That mournful day when I set sail from thee.
From thee, my fair, my own sweet Italy!
To cross the wide, the wild, tempestuous sea!

Here, in this rugged waste, I wander rude,
And lonely vigils with the wold maintain,   10
While lost, and wand'ring in dim solitude,
I urge my course along the boundless plain!

And still, my thoughts are ever turned to thee,
My own dear land, romantic Italy!
There my Aminta dwells, far o'er the sea—
O, bear me back, my star, or bear her thence to me!

Appendix:

The Poems in Order of Publication

The Literary Gazette
1. Sonnet ("I seek the fields, the woods, and gentle streams,")
   (vol. 3, 1818, p. 43)
2. Sonnet ("These days of mis'ry, loved one, for thy sake,")
   (vol. 3, 1818, p. 315)
3. Sonnet ("I seek the dark and lone retreat,")
   (vol. 3, 1818, p. 347)
4. Sonnet ("Sweet Spring, thy young and soft love-beaming
   eye") (vol. 5, 1819, p. 170)
5. Sonnet: To a Young Lady Musing (vol. 5, 1819, p. 397)
6. The Spectre (vol. 6, 1819, p. 667)
7. Sonnet: Winter (vol. 6, 1819, p. 684)
8. Sonnet: After the Ancient Style (vol. 6, 1819, p. 699)
9. Sonnet: The Poet Praises His Cat, Scracco
   (vol. 6, 1819, p. 796)
10. Sonnet: To Melancholy (vol. 6, 1819, p. 796)
11. Sonnet: To My Lamp (vol. 6, 1819, pp. 812-13)
12. Sonnet ("Vain thoughts, vain hopes, and fond desires are
    fled,") (vol. 7, 1820, p. 11)
13. Hodge (vol. 7, 1820, pp. 28-29)
14. Sonnet ("Now through the air the western breezes play,")
    (vol. 8, 1820, p. 428)
15. Sonnet ("Whilst that I wander in the pleasant fields,")
    (vol. 8, 1820, p. 445)
16. Sonnet: The Poet Laments the Death of His Cat, Scracco
    (vol. 8, 1820, p. 525)
17. Sonnet ("Whilst on the couch of pain and sorrow laid,")
    (vol. 8, 1820, p. 685)

18. Lines/Tradotto (vol. 9, 1821, p. 155)
19. Sonnet ("There came to me a poor and care-worn clerk,")
       (vol. 9, 1821, p. 332)
20. Sonnet ("I will not hurt thee, sleek and gentle mouse,")
       (vol. 10, 1821, p. 651)
21. Culloden (vol. 11, 1822, p. 169)
22. Sonnet: Written on Good Friday (vol. 11, 1822, p. 235)
23. Epigram (vol. 17, 1825, p. 92)

The Sangamo Journal
24. Hame's the Best Place A'ter A' (15 Dec. 1831, p. 3)
25. Cauld Comfort (22 Dec. 1831, p. 3)
26. To "The Prairie Bard" (12 Jan. 1832, p. 1)
27. Lines on the Approach of Winter (19 Jan. 1832, p. 3)
28. Huyler's Ghost (26 Jan. 1832, p. 2)
29. Sonnet ("How like myself in former years and now;")
       (9 Feb. 1832, p. 3)
30. Sonnet: The Poet Praises His Cat (16 Feb. 1832, p. 3)
       Reprinted from *The Literary Gazette*
31. To the Small Beer Poets (23 Feb. 1832, p. 3)
32. Lines ("Dark o'er my brow the vanished years")
       (1 Mar. 1832, p. 2)
33. Bards and Reviewers (8 Mar. 1832, pp. 2-3)
34. The Roses (15 Mar. 1832, p. 1)
35. The Western Wilds (22 Mar. 1832, p. 2)
36. Sonnet to the Frogs (29 Mar. 1832, p. 2)
37. On the Arrival of the First Steam Boat (29 Mar. 1832, p. 3)
38. Taur Arthur (12 Apr. 1832, p. 1)
39. The Remonstrance (26 Apr. 1832, p. 1)
40. On the Second Arming against Black Hawk
       (3 May 1832, p. 2)
41. Sonnet: To a Young Lady Musing (10 May 1832, p. 1)
       Reprinted from *The Literary Gazette*
42. Lines ("When I recall the days gone by,") (10 May 1832, p. 2)
43. Sonnet ("The gentle Spring, soft breathing, dropping
       flowers") (17 May 1832, p. 2)
44. The Exile (31 May 1832, p. 2)
45. L'amour Coquet (7 June 1832, p. 1)

72. Sonnet ("This vapor we call life is but a breath,")
        (12 Jan. 1839, p. 2)
73. L'envoy (12 Jan. 1839, p. 2)
74. Sonnet ("The sullen hours on leaden pinions fly,")
        (28 June 1839, p. 2)
75. The Indian (26 July 1839, p. 1)
76. The Hindoo Heaven (16 Aug. 1839, p. 4)
77. Astrology Fallacious (16 Aug. 1839, p. 4)
78. The Improvement of Modern Times (7 Sept. 1843, p. 1)
79. Sonnet ("From southern shores to Sangamo I come—")
        (1 Oct. 1845, p. 1)
80. Winter (1 Oct. 1845, p. 4)
81. The Wish (1 Oct. 1845, p. 4)
82. The Independent Philosopher (1 Oct. 1845, p. 4)
83. From the Italian (13 Nov. 1845, p. 1)
84. When Will the Spring Return? (15 Jan. 1846, p. 2)
85. Wolves (22 Jan. 1846, p. 2)
86. Written Near Springfield Church-yard (5 Feb. 1846, p. 2)
87. Content the Best Fortune (12 Feb. 1846, p. 3)
88. Le Solitaire (12 Feb. 1846, p. 1)
89. The Gods of Old (26 Feb. 1846, p. 1)
90. Sonnet ("Still lingers winter; and the blust'ring wind,")
        (26 Feb. 1846, p. 1)
91. Sonnet ("To struggle on, to struggle on for aye—")
        (26 Feb. 1846, p. 2)
92. The Approach of Spring (12 Mar. 1846, p. 2)
93. Secret Sorrow (19 Mar. 1846, p. 2)
94. L'etourdi (26 Mar. 1846, p. 3)
95. Spirits (26 Mar. 1846, p. 3)

Notes

1

Line 1. This little booke. Evidently H. prepared a collection of lyrics for which this was the opening poem. He may have sent such a collection to the editor of *The Literary Gazette,* who then chose this and other items from it for his periodical. There is no evidence that H. ever published a volume of lyrics.

3

The French headnote is from the works of Antoinette Deshoulieres (1638-1694).

Line 3. The newspaper text has "fanes" instead of "fens," but the latter is obviously what H. intended. In "Sonnet: To Melancholy," the poet also mentions wandering in the "desert fens."

5

The Italian headnote is from Petrarch's *Canzoniere,* XXXV, lines 1-2.

Line 8. The indefinite article has been added because the line is otherwise ungrammatical. It was probably omitted accidentally by the printer.

7

The headnote is from the works of William Drummond of Hawthornden (1585-1641), who was often called "the Scottish Petrarch" because of his excellent sonnets.

8

The Italian headnote from the works of Pietro Metastasio
(1698-1782) was used by the poet for three other poems:
"Vernal Musings," "The Approach of Spring," and "Son-
net" ("The gentle Spring, soft breathing, dropping flow-
ers"). The last of these is similar to the present poem.

9

The Italian headnote is from Petrarch's *Canzoniere,* CXXVI,
line 1.

11

This poem resembles lines 19-25 of "Winter Nights," which
appeared in the *Sangamo Journal* in 1837.

12

This poem was later published, with slight alterations, in the
Sangamo Journal, February 16, 1832, p. 3. Because a
Springfield poet had published a sonnet in praise of his cat a
couple weeks earlier (in an issue which does not survive), H.
decided to reprint this lyric. He signed it "Another Bache-
lor" because the other poet had signed his sonnet "A Bache-
lor." The 1832 text varies only slightly from the 1819 ver-
sion:

> 'Tis now six months and more, my whisker'd friend,
> Since first you peep'd within this narrow room,
> The gift of one who did thy worth commend
> And, thus, preserved thee from an early doom.
> Thou wast a kitten then, and gay of mind;
> With thine own tail wouldst innocently play—
> Most strangely puzzled that that thing behind
> Should still escape, turn thee which ever way.
> But now thou'rt grown a good and shapely cat,

Of aspect sage, that's seldom mov'd with ire,   10
And though, indeed, thou art not very fat,
Thou sit'st content before my little fire—
Or, purring glad, when spread our humble fare,
With gentle paw entreat'st thy slender share.

14

The source of the French headnote has not been identified.
Line 9. Jemmy. The poet added a footnote to this name: "An
acquaintance—un peu sourcilleux." The French phrase
means "a small beetle-browed person," and is evidently de-
scriptive of his dog.

15

A slightly different version of this poem appeared in the *San-
gamo Journal,* May 10, 1832, p. 1. A footnote by the poet,
indicating that it was "First published in the London Liter-
ary Gazette," led to the discovery of H's early poems. The
later text is as follows:

Thy face looks sad, fair maid, and yet that look
So sweetly doth become thy virgin brow
That one might soothly say he hath mistook,
And gazed upon an angel here below.
Is it fond love which gives that tender shade
And catcheth such soft witchey around?
Sure, love can never grieve so fair a maid,
And grief, though cruel, thee could never wound.
Perhaps thy soul, all pensive and serene,
In meditation seeks its native sky,   10
And whilst it soars beyond this mortal scene,
Imparts that seeming sorrow to the eye;
But whether love, or thought alone, it be,
It adds a grace to maiden modesty.

16

The Italian headnote is from Dante's *Inferno,* XXXIII, lines
26-27. It is also used as the headnote to poem 65.

17

For the author of the headnote, see the note to poem 7.

18

The headnote is from the works of Christopher Anstey
(1724-1805), whose *New Bath Guide* (1766) was a very popu-
lar verse satire.
Lines 8-9. Lincoln's Inn, Gray's Inn, and The Temple are refer-
ences to famous British legal societies, the Inns of Court.
Line 14. I drew out pleas. This seems to indicate that H. was at one
time connected with either the Inner Temple or the Middle
Temple. Those legal societies are located adjacent to one
another and are often spoken of together as "the Temple."

19

The battlefield at Culloden, near Inverness, Scotland, was
the scene of the bloody defeat of the Pretender Charles Ed-
ward Stuart by the Duke of Cumberland on April 16, 1746.

21

Line 19. Grey-malkin. Grimalkin was evidently the poet's favorite
name for a cat. It is also found in "The Remonstrance" (line
146) and in a sonnet ("The sullen hours on leaden pinions
fly,").
Line 27. This line is very similar to line 31 of "Lines on the Ap-
proach of Winter": "The sparkling ale with glee goes round."
Also, the subject of this part of "Hodge"—winter's indoor

pleasures— is the same as that of the later lyric, which appeared in the *Sangamo Journal* in 1832.

Lines 43-44. These two lines are very similar to lines 4 and 5 of "The Independent Philosopher": "Me heedeth not/ The world a jot." The later poem, which appeared in the *Sangamo Journal* in 1845, is also in the same six-line stanza form.

22

The six-line Italian poem is an adaptation of the couplet printed above it. The word "Tradotto" means translation, but of course, the lyric is a somewhat expanded version of the English lines. The couplet was probably traditional. H's ability to write poetry in Italian, as demonstrated here, reveals that his knowledge of that language must have been extensive.

23

The author mentioned in the headnote has not been otherwise identified. He was evidently too obscure to be referred to in French literary histories and reference works.

24

Line 1. Auld Nickieben. A colloquial name for the devil, which the poet probably borrowed from the final stanza of Burns's "Address to the Deil."

Line 3. Auld Sooty. A colloquial name for the devil.

Line 7. The final words in this line are evidently a reference to Satan's journey from Hell to Eden and his subsequent challenge to God's plans, as depicted in Milton's *Paradise Lost.* Like that famous poem, "Hame's the Best Place A'ter A'" depicts the devil's quest for a better habitation.

Line 28. polyglot. A polyglot Bible, containing versions of the same text in several languages.

Line 30. The definite article has been added both because the line

is ungrammatical without it and because another syllable is
needed if the line is to be metrically parallel with the preced-
ing one. The word was probably accidentally omitted by the
printer.

Line 34. Attic. Although the word generally means "marked by
qualities characteristic of the Athenians," in this instance it
simply means "Greek."

Line 35. Hugo Grotius (1583-1645) was a Dutch jurist and scholar
who wrote Latin works in history, philosophy, and theology,
along with a vast amount of poetry.

Line 36. John Duns Scotus (1266-1308), the "Doctor Subtilis,"
was a Franciscan friar and an influential scholastic theolo-
gian.

Line 60. Jabez Capps immigrated to the Sangamo County area of
Illinois from London in 1819. He was a shoemaker as well as
the owner of a grocery (general store and bar) in which H. was
employed.

Line 112. Mrs. Eaton. Margaret O'Neale Timberlake had a repu-
tation as a woman of easy virtue before she married her se-
cond husband, John Henry Eaton, a friend and political sup-
porter of Andrew Jackson. When the newly-elected Presi-
dent appointed Eaton as Secretary of War, Washington so-
ciety was scandalized and proceeded to snub the Eatons—
while Jackson emerged as a staunch supporter of the contro-
versial woman.

25

The headnote to the poem is taken from the headnote to
Burns's "Scotch Drink."

Line 48. se ipse. Latin for "know thyself."

26

This poem is a verse letter directed to a poet in nearby Jack-
sonville who signed his lyrics "The Prairie Bard." H. prob-
ably did not know that the poet was John Howard Bryant
(1807-1902), the youngest brother of William Cullen Bryant.

However, in the summer of 1832 William visited his brother at Jacksonville, and they traveled to Springfield. Hence, it is possible that H. met both of the Bryants.

Line 70. Pegassus. In Greek mythology, a winged horse which was the steed of the Muses and which carried poets during periods of poetic inspiration.

Line 73. Punic faith. "Punic" means characteristic of the ancient Carthagenians, from the negative perspective of the Romans, and so "Punic faith" is equivalent to faithlessness.

Line 75. the thistle. The thistle flower is the heraldic and national emblem of Scotland, and so H. was evidently of Scottish descent.

Line 113. Jacksonville is located in Morgan County, through which the Mauvaisterre River flows—a tributary of the Illinois.

27

Huyler, whose ghost appears in the poem, is otherwise unknown. His Dutch accent is indicated by the poet in spellings such as "leetle," "doomb," "waater," and "pitters." "Monongahela" refers to Monongahela whiskey, which was common on the frontier, and *"Stoughton"* refers to another kind of liquor, Stoughton's bitters.

Line 20. in propria persona. A Latin expression meaning "in his own person."

Line 46. Jabez Capps' old grocery. See the note to line 60 of poem 24.

Line 47. Rhadamanthus. In Greek mythology, a son of Zeus and Europa. For his justice on earth, he was made one of the judges of souls in the lower world after he died. In the present context, he is simply one of the devils of the vague Hell or Otherworld from which Huyler's ghost has returned.

Line 69. McKenny's clock. R. T. McKenney was a Springfield businessman whose shop was located near Jabez Capps' grocery.

28

Lines 1-2. These two lines refer to recent poems in the *Sangamo Journal* which focused on cats. H's own cat-lyric, "Sonnet: The Poet Praises His Cat," which was signed "Another Bachelor," appeared on February 16, 1832 (p. 3). The same issue also contains "To 'A Bachelor' who Boasts of Affection for 'Cats'" (p. 1), which criticizes an earlier poem (that does not survive) by "A Bachelor." Hence, the poet connects bachelors with cats in line 3 of the present poem.

Line 85. The poet added a footnote to this line: "Vide, Sonnet on Mud." This refers to a poem entitled "Sonnet on Mud" that appeared in the *Sangamo Journal* on February 16, 1832 (p. 1). That sonnet is unsigned.

Lines 88-89. The poet's recollection of the line from Byron is not very accurate. In stanza xi of the fourth canto of *Don Juan,* Byron refers to the heart as "The precious porcelain of human clay."

Line 133. jam satis—quantum suff. This mixture of French and Latin terms can be translated as "(I am) already satisfied—that much suffices."

29

Line 1. Scruter, Scrutator, Scru. "Bards and Reviewers" was written in response to a previous article in the Jacksonville *Patriot* that severely criticized the poets whose lyrics were appearing in the *Sangamo Journal.* The article does not survive, but H's poem indicates that it was signed "Scrutator," meaning "the one who scrutinizes." In this opening line the poet mentions that Latin pseudonym and the verb from which it is derived (Scruter, "to scrutinize") in the process of reducing the critic's name to a comical clipped form, *"Scru."*

Line 10. This line alludes to Horace's view—expressed in "The Art of Poetry"—that untaught genius alone does not make a poet.

Line 15. This line seems to indicate that Scrutator criticized an at-

torney-turned-poet in his article, and that H. himself had crit-
icized the same man earlier. However, the criticism of Scru-
tator does not survive, and no versifying attorney is mention-
ed in the poet's surviving satires. Of course, in the previously
published poem, "To the Small Beer Poets," H. criticized the
Springfield rhymsters in general—which is alluded to in lines
23-29 of "Bards and Reviewers."

Line 45. de gustibus non. These words are part of a Latin maxim,
"de gustibus non est disputandum": "there is no disputing
about tastes."

Line 60. Jabez Capps. See the note to line 60 of poem 24.

Line 97. Tommy Moore. Thomas Moore (1779-1852) was a popu-
lar romantic poet, satirist, and composer of the early nine-
teenth century.

Line 114. As this line indicates, "Bards and Reviewers" was writ-
ten from the point of view of one of the lesser poets ("small-
beer poets") of Springfield. This was necessary because H.
had already criticized his fellow versifiers in "To the Small
Beer Poets"—and now his purpose was to defend those same
poets from the criticism of Scrutator.

Lines 146-47. These lines indicate that someone named Tomp-
kins was encouraging poets in the Springfield area. Nothing
else is known about this individual.

Lines 152-56. These lines paraphrase *A Midsummer Night's
Dream,* v, i, 12-13.

Line 157. my brother of the prairie. This is a reference to a
Jacksonville poet who called himself The Prairie Bard. See
line 172 and the notes to "To 'The Prairie Bard.'"

Line 162. The first steamboat to navigate the Sangamon River,
The Talisman, had just arrived in Springfield. See "On the
Arrival of the First Steam Boat" and the notes to that poem.

Lines 188-89. These two lines refer to H's assertion that poetry
should be written about the Illinois countryside, in "To 'The
Prairie Bard,'" lines 85-117.

Lines 205-08. The exact lines of Butler's *Hudibras* to which the
poet is referring have not been located.

30

The occasion for this poem was the arrival in Springfield of *The Talisman,* the first steamboat to navigate the Sangamon River. Local residents were elated, for they felt that the event would usher in a new era of prosperity as river traffic for shipping purposes increased. However, the river level declined a few days later, and *The Talisman* hurried away, never to return.

Lines 1-4. The source for this reference to Jason's quest for the Golden Fleece was probably Book VII of Ovid' *Metamorphoses.*

Lines 24-25. Columbus felt, toward the end of his life, that he was not justly recognized or rewarded for his achievement by Spain's King Ferdinand. Hence, the poet is hoping that the "lot" of Pollock and Bogue will not be similar.

Line 26. Captain Pollock's name. Captain J. W. Pollock brought *The Talisman* up the Sangamon River to Springfield.

Line 29. Bogue. Vincent Bogue was a wealthy businessman of the Springfield area who sponsored the voyage of *The Talisman* up the Sangamon River.

Line 45. Suckers. Illinois residents were often called "Suckers" in the first half of the nineteenth century.

Line 70. Jackson. This is short for Jacksonville, which had several "learned men" connected with the recently-founded Illinois College.

Line 88. In other words, they were married. Hymen was the god of marriage in classical mythology.

Line 92. Prairie Bard. See "To 'The Prairie Bard'" and the notes to that poem.

Line 95. Our Bard. Lines 95-99 are a self-portrait of the poet.

Line 100. Jabez's gude liquors. See the note to line 60 of poem 24.

Line 104. Scru. Scrutator, the critic to whom "Bards and Reviewers" is directed. See the notes to that poem.

Line 105. sauve qui peut. This French phrase can be translated as "whoever can, save himself."

Lines 110-137. These lines are addressed to The Prairie Bard.

Line 121. The word "what" appears in the newspaper text of this line: "See what the western wilds I've writ on." It has been omitted in this edition because it makes the line ungrammatical and was almost certainly an error by the poet or the printer. H. is actually giving the title of his recent poem, "The Western Wilds," in this line.

Line 135. Mauvais Terre. The Mauvaisterre River flows through Morgan County near Jacksonville. Springfield and Jacksonville were rival towns in frontier Illinois.

Line 137. The steamboat which navigated the Sangamon River was called *The Talisman.*

31

Line 24. Tommy Moore. See the note to line 97 of poem 29.

Line 35. Houries. Houries were nymphs of the Mohammedan paradise, supposedly created from musk and spices, and endowed with perpetually virgin youth and perfect beauty.

Line 36. Musselmen. Mohammedans, Moslems.

32

Line 11. Scrutator. See the note to line 1 of poem 29.

Line 20. The word "it" in the newspaper text has been changed to "you" for the present edition since the poet obviously intended to make a point about the tenor rather than the vehicle of his image.

Line 31. The Journal. The *Sangamo Journal,* which had previously published verse by the small-beer poets.

Line 72. the pure Castalian stream. A spring sacred to the Muses; hence, the source of poetic inspiration.

33

The headnote refers to Mrs. Lydia Sigourney (1771-1865), of Hartford, Connecticut, who was the most popular female poet in America during the pre-Civil War period. Her lyrics

occasionally appeared in the *Sangamo Journal* and count-
less other newspapers and magazines throughout the coun-
try. Her poem entitled "The Western Emigrant" was pub-
lished on the same page of the Springfield newspaper as
"The Western Wilds" and, hence, inspired the lyric by H.—
as the headnote suggests.

34

Line 31. See the note to line 27 of poem 21.

35

Lines 19-25. The subject matter of these lines is similar to that of
"Sonnet: Winter," which appeared in *The Literary Gazette* in
1819.
Line 32. Mon'gahela. Monongahela whiskey, which was common
on the frontier. H. mentions in his preface to "Huyler's
Ghost" that it was sold in Jabez Capps's grocery.

39

On the author of the headnote, see the note to poem 8.
Line 46. Sucker. Illinois residents were often called "Suckers" in
the first half of the nineteenth century.
Line 64. a small-beer poet. One of the local poets of the Springfield
area.
Line 86. In this line, the poet is referring to the meaning that he
finds in the word "Sangamo." *Amo* is Latin for "I love."
Hence, "Sangamo" suggests something like "I love to sing, or
I love song."

40

Line 36. Titania. The wife of Oberon and queen of the fairies in
Shakespeare's *Midsummer Night's Dream.*

Line 40. Tintagel's ruin'd towers. The ruins of Tintagel Castle—the legendary home of King Arthur—are located on the northwestern coast of Cornwall, near the place where H. was raised. See "Taur Arthur."

42

For information on H's references to "the small-beer poets" and the "cat-muse," see "To the Small Beer Poets" and the note to lines 1-2 of that poem. Later in the preface to "Sonnet to the Frogs" H. refers to Leander, which was the pseudonym of another Springfield poet. He also quotes the headnote from the latter's lyric, "The Poetry of Nature" ("The world is full of poetry"), which appeared in the *Sangamo Journal* on February 9, 1832 (p. 3). For information on Jabez Capps, whose grocery is mentioned in the preface, see the note to line 60 of poem 24.

Line 10. the neighbor town. Jacksonville.

Line 13. the Scru. Scrutator, to whom "Bards and Reviewers" is addressed. See the note to line 1 of that poem.

44

On the author of the headnote, see the note to poem 8.

45

On the author of the headnote, see the note to poem 8.

48

Line 11. The letter "s" has been added to the word "play" because the line is otherwise ungrammatical. Such a mistake may have been made by either the poet or the printer.

49

Line 5. The word "is" has been added to the line for this edition. It was probably omitted accidentally by the printer.

50

The headnote, in French, is translated in the first six words of the second line of the poem. The source is unknown.

51

Concerning the author of the headnote, see the note to line 97 of poem 29.

Line 10. Saukie. The Sauk Indians possessed all of western Illinois until they were finally driven out in the Black Hawk War of 1832. However, they lived in Iowa for several years—not by the mouth of the Mississippi River, as the line implies—before moving to Oklahoma.

52

The Italian headnote is from the works of Vincenzo da Filicaia (1642-1707). It is also used as a headnote to "L'envoy" and (with slight variation) "From the Italian."

59

For the author of the headnote, see the note to poem 52.

Line 1. The past tense ending has been added to the rhyme word in this line so as to avoid the obvious awkwardness created by the present tense form, "stray."

62

Line 9. Kama. Kama (or Kamadeva) is the Hindu god of love. He is generally regarded as the son of Vishnu, but he is described in some texts as a son of Brahma.

Line 10. Siraswatta. This is a variant spelling of "Sarasvati," a fair young woman who is the wife of Brahma. She is the Hindu goddess of wisdom and learning.

Line 14. Siva. The third person of the Hindu trinity—along with Brahma, the Creator, and Vishnu, the Preserver—Siva is the Destroyer. However, since death leads into a new form of life in Hindu belief, Siva is also a regenerator or re-creator.

63

The Latin headnote is part of a proverbial expression, "Tempora mutantur, nos et mutamur in illis," which means "The times change and we change with them."

64

The title translates as "The Solitary One." The source of the French headnote is unknown.

65

The Italian headnote is from Dante's *Inferno,* XXXIII, lines 26-27. It is also used as the headnote to poem 16.

68

The French headnote is from the works of Nicolas Boileau (1636-1711).

70

The title of the poem means "Arthur's Rock" (*taur* is Cornish), and it evidently refers to High Cliff, the highest point on the Cornish seacoast. This landmark is near Tintagel Castle—the legendary home of King Arthur—on the northwest coast of Cornwall.

Line 43. Where Arthur fell. The Tintagel Castle area is the legendary location of the battle between King Arthur and Modred (his bastard son) that resulted in the destruction of the Round Table society.

Line 49. The Cymri's. The word *Cymri* means "the Welsh," which would include, in this case, the people of Cornwall.

Line 52. Caradoch's son. In Welsh mythology Caradoc was the son of Bran, the god of war and patron of bards and musicians. H. evidently associates Caradoc with these values as well. There is also a Caradoc in the Arthurian cycle of romances. He is a valiant knight of the Round Table.

Line 56. Taliessen. A legendary Welsh bard of the sixth century, who sang of Welsh warriors, including several associated with King Arthur. Some poems in a fourteenth-century manuscript have been ascribed to him. H. views him as a valiant defender of early Britain.

Line 69. Tintaggel. See the first note to this poem.

Line 76. Modred. The traitorous bastard-son of King Arthur, who seized control of the latter's kingdom and later gave him his death wound. See Book XXI of Malory's *Morte Darthur.*

71

The following notes supplement those given by the poet himself directly after the poem.

Line 1. Odin's Hall. Valhalla, Odin's banquet hall, to which slain heroes were brought, according to Norse mythology. Odin was ruler of the gods.

Line 20. Lorna's wood. This reference has not been identified.

Line 24. Thelma. This name for the scald (Norse poet) was evidently made up by H.

Line 25. Modred's bloody fight. This is apparently a reference to the battle in which King Arthur was slain. See Book XXI of Malory's *Morte Darthur.*

Lines 33-36. These lines summarize the story of "Baldr's Dreams" in *The Poetic Edda.*

Lines 37-56. These lines summarize the most famous tale in *The Poetic Edda,* "The Lay of Thrym."

Line 41. Lok. See the poet's note on this figure. The name is commonly spelled "Loki." He was the god of mischief, evil, fire, and destruction in Norse mythology.

Lines 69-80. These lines summarize "the twilight of the gods," and they are based on the "Voluspa" ("The Prophecy of the Seeres") in *The Poetic Edda.*

Line 88. Nifflema's dark and dreary shade. Nifflema—commonly spelled "Niffelheim"—was the Norse equivalent of Hell. See the poet's note.

Line 114. the frozen North. Nifflema, or Niffelheim.

Line 126. Freya. She was the goddess of love, beauty, and fertility in Norse mythology—hence,the Norse Venus. In Germany, Freya was identified with Frigg, or Frigga, the wife of Odin. H. has followed this tradition. In "The Hall of Odin," she seems to represent the principle of love or harmony, which stands opposed to the principle of conflict or discord, represented by Lok.

72

Line 10. Inds'. India's.

Line 11. Brama's mind. Brahma is the Creator in the Hindu trinity.

Line 15. Oden and Woden. These are both names for the ruler of the Norse gods. (The Norse people called him Odin; the Anglo-Saxons called him Woden.)

Line 27. Hela . . . and Fenris. The daughter of Loki, Hela (or Hel) was the Norse goddess who ruled over those who died of disease or old age. However, to H. she is simply the goddess of death. See his notes at the end of "The Hall of Odin." Fenris, the Wolf in Norse mythology, was also the offspring of Loki. At the twilight of the gods, he will devour the sun.

74

The Italian headnote is from *Gerusalemme Liberata,* XII, lxxi, 8, by Torquato Tasso (1544-1595).

75

The Italian headnote is from Petrarch's *Canzoniere,* CXXVI, line 5.

76

Line 25. Hafez. Mohammed Shams od-Din Hafez (c. 1325-1389),
known as Hafez of Shiraz, is the greatest of Persian lyric
poets. His poems are noted for their celebration of love and
wine, as well as their expression of Sufi mystical theology.

78

Line 14. the Sangamo. The Sangamon River.

79

The title of the poem seems to indicate that it is an adapta-
tion of an Italian lyric, but if so, the poet's source is unknown.
Concerning the author of the headnote, see the note to poem
52.

83

Line 6. This line is the poet's only negative comment on the Sanga-
mon River area.

85

The French title of the poem means "The Scatterbrain."

87

Line 16. Tomanoc. This is evidently an Indian word, but its mean-
ing is unknown.
Line 32. Atassi, This Indian name may have been made up by the
poet. There was no prominent Indian of this name in Black
Hawk's tribe.
Line 86. Schetabo. Probably an Indian word. The meaning is un-
known.

Line 96. Nishishin. Evidently the name of an Indian, but nothing is known about this figure.

Line 108. Ajax. One of the greatest Greek warriors in Homer's *Iliad.*

Line 109. The mighty Greek. Achilles.

Line 113. each Sucker's deeds. Illinois residents were often called "Suckers" in the first half of the nineteenth century.

Line 119. by Sangamo. By residents of Sangamon County.

Line 120. Odin's gift. The gift of poetry. See the poet's first footnote to "The Hall of Odin."

Line 121. Sucker land. Illinois.

88

James D. Henry (d. 1834), a Springfield resident, was elected Brigadier General in the Illinois militia in June of 1832. He achieved regional fame by pursuing Black Hawk's band up the Rock River and into Wisconsin and directing the Battle of Bad Axe—at which Indian men, women, and children were ruthlessly slaughtered, ending the brief Black Hawk War. See Thomas Ford, *History of Illinois* (Chicago: S. C. Griggs, 1854), pp. 124-60, and John Reynolds, *My Own Times* (1855; rpt. Chicago: Chicago Historical Society, 1879), pp. 253-65.

Line 26. The Bard. The poet is referring to himself, The Bard of Sangamo. Undoubtedly, this line summarizes the view of many Springfield residents, who were encouraging the poet to celebrate the deeds of General Henry.

Line 27. our Sangamo. Sangamon County.

89

The present mentioned in this poem was evidently sent to the poet as a result of his comic request in "To 'The Prairie Bard,'" lines 62-65.

90

The French title means "Flirtatious Love."
Lines 1-2. Collin and Chloe are conventional names for a shep-
herd and a maiden in pastoral poetry.

91

This poem is written in the same unusual stanza form as
"Hodge," and lines 5-6 are similar to lines 43-44 of that
poem.

92

The source for the Italian headnote has not been identified.

93

The Italian title translates as "The Sadness of Love." The
headnote is from the works of Pietro Metastasio (1698-
1782).

Glossary

This Glossary is largely composed of Scots terms that occur in several of the poems, but it also includes words that might be difficult for the modern reader simply because they are colloquial, archaic, or unconventionally spelled. The more easily recognizable of the poet's many contractions (such as *ev'ry, floor'd, flow'rs, slau'ter*) have been omitted. For each word listed, all the spellings are given. Names are not included, but some of them are discussed in the Notes.

a', all
aff, off
afore, before
agen, again
aiblins, perhaps
ain, own
airie, area, location
an', and
ance, once
ancien, ancien', ancient
ane, one
anither, another
ar', are
a'ter, after
a'thegither, altogether
auld, old
auld ned, see **old ned**
ava, at all, of all
awa', away
awfu', awful
aye, ever, always

bairn, child
baith, both
bardie, diminutive of *bard* (referring to the poet himself)
barton, barnyard
bedizen'd out, heavily made up and overdressed
bellyfu', bellyfull
bield, shelter
biggin, dwelling
billies, fellows, comrades
blate, modest, shy
blude, blood
bolus, a large pill
bonny, beautiful
bran' new, brand-new
braw, handsome
breeks, breeches
brimfu', brimful
brither, brother
brunstane, brimestone
buke, book
ca', call; **ca'd,** called
canna, cannot
carefu', careful
cauld, cold
certes, certainly
chiel, fellow
cholic, colic
cit, city dweller
clack, chatter
co'niac, cognac
cot, cottage
cozie, cozy
crabbit, crabbed
crack'd, talked
de'il, divel, divil, devil
ding, beat, surpass; **it dings out,** it surpasses
dinna, do not
dizens, dozens

dochters, daughters
drap, drop
dutch (the meaning is obscure); **in dutch,** for certain?
e'en, even
eke, also
enow, enough
feg, fig
fegs, faith; **I fegs,** in faith
flam, humbug, fabrication
fowk, folks; **fowk wa',** folks were
frae, from
fren', friend
frick'd, frisked
fu', full
gae, go
gat, got
gate, way, manner
gie, give
gin, if
gloamin, twilight
gude, good
ha'e, hae, have
hame, home; **hame's,** home is
handsum, handsome
haud, hold
heigh, an exclamation of surprise
hommony, hominy
hovrin', hovering
hyson-skin, tea leaves
ilka, every
ingle-nook, chimney corner
ither, other
jackus, jackass
jaw, talk
jingletry, the art of poetry
jist, just
jist, joust (i.e. do battle)
ken, know

laith, loath
lang, long; **langs,** longs; **langing,** longing
leddie, lady
levin, lightning
ligin', live in
list, listen
loo, a card game in which the taker of each trick wins a
        pool of money
lours, threatens
louvin', loving
mair, more
maist, most
mak', make
'mangst, among
maun, moen, must
meagrims, blues, low spirits
mickle, great
mixt, mixed
mony, many
moon-rakers, stupid louts
mote, may
mow, mouth
mysel', myself
na, nae, no not
naething, nothing, not at all
nane, none
nation, extremely
ne, nor
ned, see **old ned**
needna, need not
ne'er, never
neive, fist
niest, next
o', of
old ned, auld ned, bacon
ony, any
or . . . or, either . . . or

perdie, surely
phiz, slang abbreviation for physiognomy, face
pickayoon, picayune
pone, corn pone
'postle, apostle
potion, drink; **a gude potion,** a great amount
puir, poor
quiddilies, quiddities, trifling points
random-splore, chance frolic
receivit, received
roavin', plans (for traveling)
roun', round
rout, fuss, uproar
sae, so
sair, sore; **sair lang,** very long; **sairly,** sorely
sartin, certain
saul, soul
scrabble, claw about frantically
scrad, scrag, the lean end of a neck of mutton or veal
scraw'd, scrawled
serie, sorry
sheeny, shining
shoon, shoes
sic, such
smac, smack, blow
sooth, truth; **in silly sooth,** foolishly
tak', take
tauld, told
tetotum, teetotum, a small top
thegither, together
tho', though
tho't, thought
thro', through
tick, credit
trig, neatly
twa, two
unco, uncommonly

'**varsal,** universal
vera, very
wa', was; **if the fowk wa',** if the folks were
wa'd, wad, would
waes, woe is (me)
war, war', were
warld, world
weal, weel, well
wean, weans, children; **wean's,** children are
ween, believe, suppose
wha, who
wham, whom
whan, when
whar, where
whilk, which
whistle, the word is used metaphorically; **o' my whistle,**
     about myself
whoo, an exclamation expressing a swift motion
whunstane, whinestane, a name given to a curling stone
wi', with
wight, person
wiss, know
wot, know
yclept, called
ye'd, you would
ye'll, you will
ye're, you are
ye've, you have
ygret, the meaning of the word is obscure
yoursel', yourselves

Index of Titles